the art of creative altruism

REZA RIEZOUW

the art of creative altruism

A Philosophy of Creativity, Care
and Cooperation in a Shifting World

REZA RIEZOUW

ALTRUIA PRESS

CREATIVE ALTRUISM is creativity, care and cooperation working together for the greater good.

In this book, the term refers to an orientation toward creative action in which human ingenuity is guided by relational awareness, ethical responsibility, and shared purpose. It does not describe a programme or ideology, but language for practices that embed care and cooperation into the way individuals, organisations, and systems create. This definition is descriptive rather than prescriptive.

CONTENTS

Foreword   11

Creative Altruism as Literacy   15

Naming the Altruian Age   19

PART I — The Turning

From transition and turbulence toward a new pattern of creative cooperation.

Chapter 1 – The Last Tides of Pisces   27

Chapter 2 – The Quickening of Aquarius   31

Chapter 3 – From Competition to Creative Cooperation   35

Chapter 4 – Creative Altruism and the Creative Industries   39

Chapter 5 – Altruism, Creativity, and the New Evolutionary Drivers   43

Chapter 6 – The Power of Shared Belief   47

Chapter 7 – Truth, Trust, and the Courage to See   51

Chapter 8 – Empathy Beyond Pain   55

Chapter 9 – The Joyful Impulse Behind the Altruian Age   59

PART II — The Reorientation

Clarifying first principles and the inner architecture of Creative Altruism.

Chapter 10 – Thresholds, Temples, and the Everyday Sacred   65

Chapter 11 – Field Listening & Silence Keeping   69

Chapter 12   Terms, Topology, and First Principles   75

Chapter 13 – Commitments, Agreements, and the Altruian Ethic   81

Chapter 14 – The Seven Rays   89

Chapter 15 – Integration   97

Chapter 16 – Living the Rhythm   103

PART III — The Embodiment

Living Creative Altruism across individuals, teams and communities.

Chapter 17 – The Individual Path ... 111

Chapter 18 – The Team Path ... 117

Chapter 19 – The Community Path ... 123

Chapter 20 – Practices & Patterns of Creative Altruism ... 127

Chapter 21 – Playful Cooperation ... 131

Chapter 22 – Breakdowns and Breakthroughs ... 135

Chapter 23 – Wayfinding ... 141

Chapter 24 – Stories and Transmission ... 147

Chapter 25 – Transmission in Action ... 151

PART IV — Toward the Altruian Age

Extending Creative Altruism into culture, systems, economy and the future.

Chapter 26 – The Altruian Field ... 157

Chapter 27 – The Spiritual and Inner Framework ... 161

Chapter 28 – Integration and Continuity ... 165

Chapter 29 – Futures of Altruia ... 169

Chapter 30 – Scaling Without Losing Soul ... 175

Chapter 31 – Technology and the Soul of Scale ... 179

Chapter 32 – From Creative Altruism to Digital Creative Altruism ... 183

Chapter 33 – Economies of Shared Purpose ... 187

Chapter 34 – Economy as Ecology ... 193

Chapter 35 – Ageing with Purpose ... 197

Chapter 36 – Cool, Kind & Joyful ... 203

Chapter 37 – Culture and the Art of Harmony ... 209

Chapter 38 – The Spiritual Present ... 213

Chapter 39 – The Quiet Continuation ... 217

Chapter 40 – The Book, the Ecosystem, and the Invitation ... 221

Afterword – What Continues   225

Appendix – Defining Creative Altruism   227

About the Author   231

Glossary of Key Terms   235

Foreword

This book begins with a simple feeling many people recognise, even if they don't always name it.

A sense that the way we work, compete, produce, and relate to one another no longer quite fits the world we are living in — or the people we are becoming.

For some, this shows up as burnout. For others, as frustration, loss of meaning, or quiet unease. We may be busy, productive, and outwardly successful, yet still feel that something essential is missing. Something human.

The Art of Creative Altruism was written from within that question.

It does not begin with the assumption that people are selfish by nature, nor that they must be morally instructed to behave better. It also does not assume that markets, technology, or competition are inherently harmful. Instead, it asks a different question altogether:

What if care for others, creativity, and cooperation are not merely idealistic notions, but human capacities waiting to be better understood and more consciously applied?

For much of modern history, altruism has been framed as sacrifice — as something that stands in opposition to ambition, success, or freedom. This book challenges that framing. It explores altruism as something creative, intelligent, and voluntary: a way of acting that can enrich individuals, organisations, and societies at the same time.

This is not a book of moral instruction, and it is not a manifesto. It does not ask the reader to adopt an ideology or follow a prescribed path. Instead, it offers a new way of seeing — a perspective that helps make sense of cooperation, shared purpose, leadership, technology, and value creation in a shifting world.

You will not find step-by-step formulas here. What you will find are ideas, reflections, and frameworks designed to be lived with rather than consumed. The intention is not to tell you what to think, but to create space for new kinds of thinking to emerge.

The world we are navigating today is complex. Economic systems are strained, trust is fragile, technology is advancing faster than our cultural frameworks can keep up, and many people feel caught between cynicism and idealism. This book does not deny those realities. It meets them calmly and honestly — without fear, and without false promises.

It also treats technology, including artificial intelligence, as neither saviour nor threat, but as a mirror of human intention. Tools amplify what we bring to them. The deeper question, therefore, is not what our technologies can do, but what we choose to do together.

At its heart, *The Art of Creative Altruism* is an invitation.

An invitation to reconsider how we define success.
An invitation to rethink how we collaborate and compete.
An invitation to explore how creativity and care can become practical forces in everyday life and work.

You do not need to agree with everything in these pages. This book was written to be approached with curiosity rather than certainty. If some of these ideas feel unfamiliar at first, that is fine — the book is designed to unfold slowly.

If it helps you see your work, your relationships, or your role in the world a little more clearly — and a little more generously — then it has done what it set out to do.

Creative Altruism as Literacy

Creative Altruism is often mistaken for a personal disposition—a matter of kindness, generosity, or moral preference. This misunderstanding is understandable. For much of modern history, altruism has been framed as character rather than capacity, and creativity as talent rather than infrastructure. Yet what is emerging now asks for a different framing.

Creative Altruism is not a trait.
It is a literacy.

A literacy is a way of reading reality and responding intelligently to it. It is not innate virtue, but learnable capacity. Literacy allows participation. It enables people to move within complexity without being overwhelmed by it. It turns instinct into skill and goodwill into practice.

Seen this way, Creative Altruism names the capacity to work creatively, caringly, and cooperatively inside complex human systems—systems shaped by speed, interdependence, technology, and consequence. It is the ability to sense what is happening in a field, recognise what is needed next, and act in ways that strengthen coherence rather than fragment it.

Just as textual literacy allows people to recognise meaning in symbols, Creative Altruism allows people to recognise patterns in relationship. It sharpens attention to tone, timing, power, and consequence. It makes visible what often goes unnoticed: when cooperation is thinning, when care has become performative, when creativity is being extracted rather than supported, when systems are optimising at the cost of humanity.

Without this literacy, people rely on rules, roles, or ideology. With it, they rely on discernment.

Creative Altruism as literacy does not replace expertise. It complements it. Technical skill remains essential. Strategy remains necessary. But without relational literacy, technical competence can accelerate harm. Creativity without care destabilises. Care without intelligence overwhelms. Cooperation without structure collapses. Literacy is what allows these forces to remain in conversation.

This literacy operates across scales.

At the individual level, it appears as the capacity to pause, listen inwardly, and act without self-fragmentation. People become able to notice when their actions are misaligned with their values and to correct course without drama.

At the team level, literacy shows up as the ability to sense and steward the field. Teams learn to recognise when tension carries information rather than threat, when disagreement can be integrated rather than avoided, and when clarity or care is needed more than speed.

At the organisational and systemic level, Creative Altruism as literacy becomes design intelligence. Leaders and designers learn to recognise how structures shape behaviour, how incentives train culture, and how defaults carry ethics. Decisions are evaluated not only by efficiency or outcome, but by their impact on dignity, learning, and long-term coherence.

Literacy changes what is considered competent.

In extractive systems, competence is measured by control, speed, and optimisation. In literate systems, competence includes restraint, timing, repair, and the ability to hold difference without collapse. This does not make systems slower. It makes them more adaptive.

Creative Altruism as literacy also reframes responsibility. Responsibility shifts from moral burden to participatory awareness. People recognise that neutrality is an illusion—every action, design choice, and omission shapes the field others must live within. Literacy makes this visible without moralising it. Responsibility becomes responsiveness.

This literacy cannot be taught through instruction alone. Like all literacies, it develops through practice, feedback, and immersion. People learn it by noticing what works, by reflecting on breakdowns, by experimenting with different ways of cooperating, and by observing the effects of their choices on others and on the system as a whole.

Over time, what once required effort becomes instinct.

The importance of this literacy becomes clear as complexity increases. In environments shaped by rapid change, automation, and global interdependence, rule-based ethics fail quickly. What is needed instead is situational intelligence—an ability to sense, adapt, and respond with care under conditions where certainty is unavailable.

Creative Altruism as literacy provides this capacity. It does not tell people what to believe. It teaches them how to pay attention. It does not impose behaviour. It cultivates discernment. It does not promise harmony. It makes cooperation workable.

As more people acquire this literacy, culture shifts quietly. What once felt idealistic becomes practical. What once required enforcement becomes normal. Cooperation stops feeling fragile and begins to feel like common sense.

Creative Altruism matters now not because the world needs more good intentions, but because it needs more people who can read complex human systems and respond with creativity, care, and cooperation—reliably, humbly, and without needing to be told what to do.

A more formal clarification of this definition appears in the Appendix.

Naming the Altruian Age

There comes a point in any cultural transition when language must catch up with experience—not to define it prematurely, but to give orientation to something already felt. Naming, as it is used here, is not an act of authority or prediction. It is an act of listening: an attempt to notice what qualities are becoming necessary, what assumptions are loosening, and what ways of being are quietly gaining ground. The term *Altruian Age* is introduced in this spirit—not as a claim about history or destiny, but as a provisional lens for recognising a cluster of shifts explored throughout this book.

It does not claim the arrival of a new era in any absolute sense. Ages do not change on schedule, nor do they replace one another cleanly. They overlap. They echo. They coexist for long stretches of time. The Altruian Age names a shift in emphasis rather than a historical rupture—a movement from extraction toward contribution, from dominance toward cooperation, from isolated intelligence toward shared intelligence.

Throughout history, ages have often been named after what they privileged: conquest, belief, reason, industry, information. Each brought extraordinary advances, and each carried costs that only became visible later. The qualities now emerging do not negate what came before. They respond to its limits.

In a world shaped by deep interdependence, unilateral power loses effectiveness. In accelerated environments, reaction becomes dangerous. Under these conditions, qualities once considered secondary—care, empathy, cooperation, ethical restraint—reveal themselves as structural necessities.

The Altruian Age names this reversal of priority.

It suggests a context in which altruism is no longer framed as sacrifice or moral heroism, but as intelligent participation in systems that can sustain themselves. Altruism here is not opposed to self-interest. It recognises that self-interest has become relational—that what undermines the whole eventually undermines the part.

This does not make people kinder as such.
It makes kindness practical.

The *Altruian* is not a new identity or category of person. It describes a mode of participation—a way of standing inside systems with awareness of consequence, dignity, and relationship. An Altruian acts with an understanding that neutrality is illusory, that every action shapes the field others must live within, and that coherence is something one contributes to, not something one demands.

The Altruian Age is therefore not defined by ideology, geography, or affiliation. It is defined by capacity. Wherever people are able to cooperate across difference, design for fairness rather than extraction, hold truth without weaponising it, and remain human under pressure, the Altruian Age is already present.

This presence is uneven. It advances and recedes. It appears in fragments—within teams, communities, platforms, and moments of collective intelligence. It is not yet dominant. But it is recognisable.

Naming this age is not an attempt to predict the future. It is an attempt to give coherence to the present. Without language, emerging qualities remain diffuse. With careful language, they become visible enough to be protected, practised, and refined.

The Altruian Age does not ask to be believed in.
It asks to be noticed.

It can be felt in shifts of tone rather than policy, in changed assumptions rather than declarations, in what begins to feel outdated rather than in what is newly fashionable. Aggression loses glamour. Exploitation loses legitimacy. Cooperation, care, and quiet integrity begin to feel not naïve, but competent.

This shift is cultural before it is institutional. It lives in how people choose to work together, how leaders hold power, how systems distribute value, how technology is shaped, and how inner life is integrated with outer action.

The Altruian Age names a context in which Creative Altruism becomes legible—not as a personal virtue, but as a literacy required to navigate complexity without collapse. What matters is not the term itself, but the quality of participation it points toward—a way of being that recognises that in a deeply connected world, the most intelligent act is often the most relational one.

The Altruian Age is not something we are waiting for.
It is something we are already learning how to live.

If we are indeed entering what might be called the Altruian Age, this naming is not a proclamation but a recognition. It does not declare that the work is done, nor that a new era has fully arrived. It simply acknowledges a quiet but growing shift — a movement toward integrating creativity with care, and individual agency with shared responsibility. To name the horizon is not to possess it, but to orient ourselves toward it. What remains is not certainty, nor a finished vision, but a widening invitation — the quiet possibility of living as though such an age were already beginning to unfold among us.

PART I

The Turning

FROM TRANSITION AND TURBULENCE TOWARD A
NEW PATTERN OF CREATIVE COOPERATION.

*What follows begins by noticing how one way of understanding meaning and
participation quietly gives way to another — not through rupture,
but through completion.*

CHAPTER 1

The Last Tides of Pisces

When an Era Learns How to Let Go

There are moments when something long familiar begins to loosen its hold. Nothing dramatic announces the change. Life continues outwardly much as before, yet a quiet misfit grows beneath the surface. Words that once carried weight feel thinner. Gestures that once felt meaningful begin to feel heavy with repetition. Many people recognise this sensation before they have language for it — as a subtle knowing that something has completed its work, and that a different way of standing in life is beginning to ask for attention.

This is not collapse. It is completion.

Creative Altruism does not arrive here to reject what came before; it begins by noticing a reorientation already underway. What once organised life through surrender gradually seeks expression through participation. Meaning does not disappear; it relocates. Authority shifts to the relational, from obedience to alignment. The question is no longer how faithfully one can submit, but how honestly one can stand in relationship with what is real.

For a long time, humanity lived within an orientation shaped by surrender and faith. Trust was placed in higher authority. Worth was often measured through sacrifice. Meaning was secured through devotion, obedience, and the willingness to yield the self to something larger. These qualities were not errors. They answered the needs of their time. To recognise this is not to judge the past, but to understand how meaning evolves. In eras marked by fear, hardship, and uncertainty, they offered coherence, endurance, and solace.

The imprint of this orientation remains. It lives quietly in habits of self-doubt and reflexes of submission. It appears in the hope that someone else knows better, in the belief that goodness requires self-erasure, in the assumption that truth arrives from above rather than emerging through lived discernment. For centuries, this posture shaped inner life and outer civilisation alike, providing stability where little else was available.

And then, slowly, it began to tire.

The language of ages used here draws from a long-standing symbolic framework rather than a literal chronology. In astrological terms, the movement from one age to another is associated with the *precession of the equinoxes*—a slow astronomical shift caused by the gentle wobble of the Earth's axis. Over approximately 26,000 years, this wobble causes the point of the spring equinox to move gradually backward through the constellations of the zodiac, spending roughly two millennia in each.

Cultures across history have used these long cycles as a way of naming broad shifts in collective orientation—how meaning is sought, how authority is understood, and how relationship is organised. The Age of Pisces has often been associated symbolically with faith, surrender, devotion, and hierarchical mediation of meaning. The Age of Aquarius, by contrast, is commonly used as a symbolic shorthand for themes of participation, shared intelligence, decentralisation, and relational awareness.

These associations are not presented here as predictions or doctrines, but as *descriptive metaphors*—a language for noticing patterns that many people recognise intuitively in cultural, psychological, and organisational life. The usefulness of this language lies not in belief, but in orientation: it helps articulate why certain ways of being begin to feel complete, and why others quietly begin to ask for expression.

In this sense, the closing of one age and the opening of another does not mark an abrupt change, but a long overlap—a gradual rebalancing of emphasis.

What is felt now is not rebellion, but fatigue. A weariness with forms that ask for loyalty without relationship. A growing discomfort with hierarchies that demand trust without accountability. People sense this before they articulate it. It appears as quiet resistance, as the recognition that something once sacred no longer carries life in the same way.

What loosens is not faith, but faith placed outside the living human being. What recedes is not meaning, but the belief that meaning must be mediated through fixed structures, distant authorities, or inherited certainties. As this confidence fades, something else begins to stir: a willingness to trust lived experience, relational truth, and inner alignment as sources of guidance.

The tide does not withdraw violently. It recedes gently, leaving behind what still nourishes and washing away what has grown rigid. In this retreat, a shoreline becomes visible again—clear enough for something new to approach. What appears is not a command, but a threshold.

Here, the impulse to surrender begins to transform. It begins to ask for participation, presence, and responsibility. The question shifts quietly but decisively—from what must be given up to be worthy, to how one might live in alignment with what feels true.

This shift unfolds privately, inside countless lives, as people begin trusting their own capacity to sense meaning rather than receiving it second-hand. The last tides of Pisces carry this movement forward gently, making room for something else to learn how to arrive.

Quiet Reprise
Some endings do not ask
to be marked.
They soften.
They recede.
They leave behind
what still belongs
and clear the ground
for a different way
of standing
inside meaning.

CHAPTER 2

The Quickening of Aquarius

When Life Begins to Move Faster Than Thought

Something has begun to move more quickly. Not only events, but experience itself. Time feels denser, as though days carry more weight than they once did. Actions return consequences before there has been time to fully prepare for them. Life no longer unfolds in clean sequences. It overlaps, compresses, and responds.

People sense this first in their bodies. Breath shortens without obvious cause. Attention scatters. A low hum of urgency persists even in moments meant for rest. It becomes harder to separate one conversation from the next, one role from another, one day from the last. Experience thickens. What once arrived gradually now presses close.

Acceleration is often mistaken for speed, but what is felt here is compression. There is less distance between intention and outcome, less delay between action and consequence. Choices ripple outward sooner than expected. What is ignored returns quickly. What is postponed accumulates. What is denied expresses itself elsewhere.

This pressure does not feel imposed from outside. It feels intrinsic, as though life itself has become more responsive. Systems answer back more quickly. Relationships register impact sooner.

Attention is the first to feel the strain. It is pulled in many directions at once, not only by demand, but by connection. Signals multiply. Context shifts mid-thought. People learn to hold several realities simultaneously and feel the cost of doing so. Everything touches everything else. Nothing stays isolated for long.

Yet within this strain, something else becomes visible. Attention, when gathered, becomes extraordinarily powerful. A brief pause can stabilise an entire exchange. A moment of presence can alter the direction of a conversation. People begin to sense that attention is no longer optional. It has become structural.

Interconnectedness, once discussed as an idea, is now encountered through consequence. A decision made in one place alters conditions elsewhere. A tone carried into one conversation shapes the field of the next. Care or carelessness travels further than expected. Relationships reveal this quickly. Nothing stands alone.

Interconnectedness demonstrates itself repeatedly until denial becomes impractical. What was once abstract now feels intimate. Systems are no longer distant forces operating in the background. They shape daily experience directly. Processes affect dignity. Structures influence mood. Design decisions touch the nervous system.

People feel when systems support them. They also feel when systems extract from them. Under these conditions, responsibility can no longer be deferred. Structure is no longer neutral. Outcomes are not accidental. Awareness arises not as ideology, but as necessity.

As complexity increases, individual certainty weakens. No single perspective holds the whole. No one can see far enough alone. This is felt not as failure, but as invitation. In conversations where listening replaces defence, intelligence begins to appear between people. Ideas build rather than collide. Insight arrives that no one brought fully formed.

Creativity, in this sense, is rarely the product of isolated insight. It emerges between people, through shared attention, trust, and the subtle coordination of differences. Creative Altruism begins here — not with individual brilliance, but with the relational conditions that allow something new to arise.

This shared intelligence is not mystical. It is relational. It becomes accessible when attention steadies and the need to dominate relaxes. The quickening rewards connection that can think.

Before concepts catch up, the body adapts. People learn to slow internally even as life accelerates externally. Presence reveals itself not as the opposite of movement, but as its regulator. Listening sharpens. Response begins to replace reaction. This is not technique. It is adjustment.

Awareness, under these conditions, ceases to be aspirational. It becomes practical. Without it, acceleration overwhelms. Interconnectedness fragments into noise. Shared intelligence collapses into confusion. Awareness here is not moral vigilance. It is sensitivity to what is happening now—inside oneself, between people, and across situations.

People discover that awareness saves energy. It prevents unnecessary damage. It allows correction before crisis. It becomes the difference between being carried by movement and being scattered by it.

Those who begin to live this way notice something unexpected. Life does not slow down. But it becomes more workable. Even in density, there are pauses that matter. Even in speed, there is room to choose tone, timing, and care.

Quiet Reprise
Life is moving.
Attention gathers.
Connection tightens.
Consequence arrives sooner.
Within the motion,
there is a way of standing—
present enough
to sense where things are going
before they arrive.

CHAPTER 3

From Competition to Creative Cooperation

When Survival Gives Way to Maturity

Competition once made sense. It sharpened attention, clarified threat, and organised effort around survival. In environments shaped by scarcity and visible danger, rivalry offered focus and speed. It answered an essential question: how do we endure?

Much of what humanity built still carries this logic within it. People learned to compare themselves. Systems learned to rank. Progress was measured by outpacing others, securing position, winning ground. Pressure produced results. Rivalry created momentum. For a long time, this orientation worked well enough. Yet what serves survival does not always serve maturity.

Over time, something subtle begins to change. The same strategies that once delivered clarity start to produce fatigue. Competition no longer sharpens; it exhausts. Speed no longer clarifies; it fragments. Advantage no longer stabilises systems; it shifts instability elsewhere. Effort increases, but effectiveness declines.

Nothing dramatic announces this shift. It appears quietly, as repetition without renewal. Teams compete internally and lose coherence. Organisations optimise relentlessly and drain the energy they depend on. Communities fracture under constant comparison. The strain is not ideological. It is practical.

Competition has not become wrong. It has simply become insufficient.

In a world of increasing complexity, survival alone is no longer an adequate organising principle. Problems no longer arrive one at a time. They overlap, amplify, and interact. No single actor holds enough perspective to respond effectively. Winning in one area often creates fragility in another.

People sense this intuitively. They notice that protecting position can undermine purpose. That securing advantage can cost trust. That rivalry, when made primary, erodes the very conditions required for anything meaningful to last. Quietly, the guiding question begins to shift—from how to win, to how to move forward together without collapsing what holds us.

Rivalry thrives on separation. It assumes clear boundaries, isolated actors, and measurable victories. But in tightly connected systems, separation is largely an illusion. Actions reverberate. Costs travel. Outcomes loop back. What appears as individual success often carries collective consequence.

This becomes visible when competition between departments stalls shared work, when rivalry between organisations fragments entire ecosystems, when personal comparison drains creativity rather than inspiring it. The energy required to sustain constant rivalry becomes greater than the systems can afford.

And so cooperation begins to appear—not as an ideal, but as a response.

People start sharing information earlier because withholding slows everything down. They listen more carefully because misunderstanding escalates quickly. They coordinate because duplication wastes time and energy they no longer have. No one calls this moral progress. They call it what works.

Cooperation emerges as intelligence under constraint.

What appears is not consensus or sameness. Differences remain. Disagreements persist. Perspectives diverge. What changes is the relationship between them. Instead of cancelling one another out, differences begin to inform. Instead of competing for dominance, ideas are arranged. Instead of forcing agreement, people learn how to work with tension.

This is creative cooperation.

Here, each contribution retains its character. Each voice keeps its timbre. The whole gains range rather than uniformity. No one is asked to surrender their edge. They learn how to place it. Difference stops being a threat and becomes a resource.

In moments of genuine cooperation, something becomes noticeable. Work feels lighter. Solutions arrive that no one planned. Energy circulates instead of draining. People recognise this immediately—not as sentiment, but as efficiency at a higher level. Intelligence is no longer trapped inside individuals. It begins to move between them.

Creative cooperation reduces wasted effort. It shortens feedback loops. It allows learning to compound rather than reset with every disagreement.

Competition does not disappear in this shift. It changes role. It moves inward—into standards, craft, discipline, and excellence. People compete with their own habits, their own limitations, their own previous work.

The sharpness remains, but it is no longer aimed at others.

What fades is competition as the primary organiser of relationship. What remains is discernment.

Those living through this transition rarely announce it. They simply stop investing energy where it no longer returns value. They choose environments where cooperation is possible. They leave systems that mistake pressure for productivity. There is no triumph here, no declaration of victory. Only recognition.

Something has stopped working. Something else is already underway.

Quiet Reprise
Competition taught us how to survive.
Cooperation is teaching us how to stay whole.
Not by agreement,
but by arrangement.
Not by softness,
but by intelligence placed well.
What emerges is not victory,
but a steadier way
of moving together.

CHAPTER 4

Creative Altruism and the Creative Industries

When Creativity Begins to Feel Unsupported

Creative work carries a particular intimacy. It emerges from attention, sensitivity, and risk before it ever becomes visible. Those who live inside creative processes recognise this immediately. They feel when work is alive, and they feel when it is being pushed too early, shaped too harshly, or extracted before it has had time to form.

Much of contemporary creative life unfolds inside systems that admire creativity without understanding it. Praise is often generous. Opportunity is frequently promised. Yet the conditions that allow creative intelligence to remain healthy are thinner than they appear. The work is celebrated; the process is rarely protected.

This produces a quiet strain.

Many creatives recognise the pattern without needing to name it. Periods of deep engagement followed by long stretches of uncertainty. Moments of recognition that do not translate into stability. The work continues, often sustained by personal resilience rather than structural support. From the outside, this adaptability is admired. From the inside, it can feel like constant negotiation with insecurity.

Creatives learn to self-manage, self-promote, self-justify. They become flexible, resourceful, and resilient. These qualities are praised as virtues, yet they often develop as responses to imbalance rather than expressions of choice. The strain is rarely acknowledged directly. It shows up as exhaustion that does not resolve with rest, as a dulling of joy, as the sense that something essential is being asked to survive in conditions that do not nourish it.

Creative systems tend to reward what is visible. Finished work. Metrics. Moments of success. What remains largely unseen is the process that makes those outcomes possible—the time, uncertainty, collaboration, and emotional labour required to bring something into being.

When systems overlook process, creatives feel it immediately. Ideas are rushed before they are ready. Collaboration becomes transactional. Risk is encouraged rhetorically and punished practically.

One of the most corrosive effects of this environment is misattribution. Creative work rarely emerges alone. It develops through influence, dialogue, shared effort, and exchange. Yet recognition often collapses toward the most visible figure or the most powerful intermediary. Contributions that are partial, supportive, or process-based slip from view.

Over time, value drains. Credit becomes unstable. Trust weakens. People stop expecting fairness and begin protecting themselves instead. This response is not bitterness. It is adaptation. But adaptation has a cost.

Uncertainty becomes a background condition long before it is acknowledged as such. It shapes which risks feel safe to take, which truths feel speakable, which projects feel viable. It narrows choice without appearing to. Many creatives carry this uncertainty silently, accepting instability as the price of expression while sensing that something deeper is misaligned.

Creative intelligence thrives on openness. Uncertainty encourages contraction.

When systems strain, responsibility is often displaced onto individuals. Creatives are asked to be more adaptable, more entrepreneurial, more resilient—as though structural imbalance were a personal shortcoming. Most comply. They learn new skills, expand roles, stretch further. Yet the feeling remains that no amount of effort can stabilise the ground.

The problem is not insufficient commitment. It is misalignment.

Creativity does not function well in isolation. It depends on trust, reciprocity, time, and shared care. It requires environments capable of holding uncertainty without panic and difference without domination. When these conditions are present, creativity sustains itself. When they are absent, no amount of talent compensates.

Creative Altruism appears here not as theory, but as recognition. Creativity needs structures that understand its nature—structures that protect process, honour contribution, and allow value to return to those who generate it. This is not idealism. It is necessity.

Across creative fields, people are already sensing this mismatch. They are gravitating toward cooperative models, shared ownership, transparent attribution, and more humane rhythms of work. Not because these approaches feel virtuous, but because they feel workable. Alignment begins to matter more than scale. Continuity more than exposure. Relationship more than profit.

This shift is uneven and incomplete, but it is real. It does not announce itself as reform. It unfolds as preference.

Creative Altruism enters this space not as a demand placed on creatives, but as a correction asked of systems. It suggests that creativity flourishes where contribution is recognised, where care is embedded, and where success does not depend on depletion. It reframes creative work not as a resource to be mined, but as a living intelligence that responds to how it is treated.

When alignment appears, tension eases. Not because work becomes easy, but because it becomes sustainable.

Quiet Reprise
Creativity knows
when it is being held
and when it is being spent.
When systems learn to listen
to what creative work requires,
strain begins to soften—
and correction becomes possible
without force.
Something does not need
to be fixed.
It needs
to be held
differently.

CHAPTER 5

Altruism, Creativity, and the New Evolutionary Drivers

When Life Learns How to Move With Itself

There are times when life begins to organise differently. Not through announcement or upheaval, but through a quiet shift in what feels workable. Effort alone no longer carries things forward. Speed without care introduces instability. Innovation without context creates more problems than it resolves. The familiar ways of pushing begin to strain, and in that strain, a different quality becomes perceptible.

Purpose starts to change its character.

It no longer announces itself as ambition or future outcome. It appears as coherence in the present moment. People feel it when their actions stop pulling against their values, when decisions no longer require constant self-justification. Purpose becomes less about where one is going and more about how one is standing. It is recognised not as aspiration, but as alignment.

This recognition brings relief. Inner and outer life begin to speak the same language.

Alongside this shift, care reveals an intelligence that has long been underestimated. Treated for generations as sentiment rather than capacity, care now shows itself as one of the most stabilising forces available to complex systems. Care stabilises relationship, preserves energy and allows learning to continue under pressure.

This is not softness. It is competence. Care, when structural rather than ornamental, reduces friction and prevents collapse. It keeps systems responsive instead of brittle.

Creativity, too, begins to mature. Novelty alone no longer satisfies. Disruption for its own sake feels hollow. Creative intelligence starts to orient toward connection. It senses context, anticipates consequence, and works with what already exists rather than against it.

This is creativity that has learned restraint without losing vitality. Imagination remains alive, but it is placed in relationship with responsibility. Creativity grows up not by becoming cautious, but by becoming situated.

These movements—purpose as coherence, care as intelligence, creativity as relational—signal a deeper shift in how evolution itself is understood. Progress no longer feels linear or directional. It feels relational. Change emerges when parts learn how to work together rather than compete for dominance, when intelligence circulates instead of concentrating, when systems adapt through responsiveness rather than force.

Evolution here is not about arrival.
It is about fit.

As these forces begin to align, momentum changes quality. Things still move, but with less strain. Decisions still occur, but without fragmentation. Effort remains, yet it is no longer constantly expended against resistance. People recognise this immediately, often without language. They say things like, *"It feels right."* These are not emotional reactions. They are perceptions of coherence.

In this context, altruism appears differently. Not as moral preference. Not as sacrifice. But as evolutionary fit. When systems are designed so that contribution strengthens the whole, altruism ceases to feel heroic. It becomes practical. It becomes the behaviour that allows complexity to remain livable.

Altruism, here, is not about giving more. It is about aligning contribution with continuity—ensuring that what is offered does not deplete the conditions that make offering possible. This alignment allows energy to circulate rather than drain, learning to compound rather than reset.

None of this is theoretical. People encounter it already in fragments: moments when collaboration suddenly flows, when leadership steadies rather than dominates, when work feels meaningful without being exhausting. These moments do not announce a new era. They simply reveal what works. And what works begins to repeat.

What emerges is not revolution, but recalibration. A balancing of forces that had grown out of proportion. A return to relationship where isolation dominated. A slowing where acceleration exhausted. Life does not abandon what brought it this far. It refines it.

Quiet Reprise
Evolution does not rush.
It listens.
When purpose aligns,
when care holds,
and when creativity connects,
life finds its balance—
not by moving faster,
but by learning how to move
with itself.

CHAPTER 6

The Power of Shared Belief

When Meaning Becomes a Field

Belief is often spoken about as something people hold—an idea, a conviction, a position taken in the mind. Yet lived experience suggests something quieter and more pervasive. Belief is encountered before it is named. It is felt in rooms, in teams, in communities—in how safe it feels to speak, in how carefully disagreement is handled, in whether effort seems to matter.

Belief announces itself as atmosphere.

Most people recognise this immediately. They enter a space and sense what is possible there before a word is spoken. Whether questions are welcome. Whether mistakes will be met with curiosity or consequence. Whether care is genuine or ornamental. Nothing is explained, yet everything is communicated. Belief lives in this unspoken layer. It is the shared understanding of how things work here—not as policy, but as expectation carried in the body.

In many environments, belief weakens without drama. Values are stated but not enacted. Purpose is displayed but not consulted. Language promises coherence while behaviour suggests otherwise. This gap rarely provokes confrontation. It produces caution. Energy becomes guarded. People stop offering what is most alive in them and begin doing what is required, no more.

Trust does not collapse.
It erodes.

Belief becomes most visible under strain. When time is short. When stakes are high. When outcomes matter. In these moments, what is truly held comes forward. Does care remain present? Does fairness hold? Is truth welcomed even when inconvenient? People watch closely, often without conscious intent. They learn what is safe to trust not from declarations, but from response.

Shared belief does not require sameness. People can disagree strongly and still move together when they trust the field. They can hold different perspectives without fragmenting when they sense a shared orientation beneath the surface. This orientation is not ideological. It is relational. It lives in how people return to one another after tension, in whether repair is possible, in whether dignity is protected when views diverge.

Belief, in this sense, is not consensus.
It is coherence.

Belief travels through behaviour. How leaders listen when challenged. How credit is shared. How mistakes are handled. Over time, behaviour becomes expectation. Expectation becomes culture. Belief settles into the field and begins to carry the work forward.

Where belief is coherent, something relaxes. People speak more freely. Creative risk becomes tolerable. Energy circulates instead of pooling. Decisions feel cleaner—not because disagreement disappears, but because disagreement no longer threatens belonging. Difficulty remains, but it becomes workable.

Where belief fragments, systems compensate. Rules multiply. Oversight increases. Control replaces trust. These measures may stabilise outcomes temporarily, but they drain life from the field. People comply outwardly and withdraw inwardly. The system continues. The spirit leaves.

Shared belief becomes most valuable as change accelerates. In uncertainty, people look for something steady—not certainty, but orientation. A sense that there is a way of moving together even when outcomes are unclear. Shared belief provides this continuity. It allows action without constant instruction, trust in one another's judgement, and adjustment without panic.

Belief, when lived, becomes invisible infrastructure.

As used here, shared belief does not require agreement or certainty. It requires a shared respect for reality. When reality can be named without fear, relationship becomes possible again. No one needs to agree on everything. They need to sense that what matters is held—that care is not conditional, that truth can be spoken, that responsibility is shared. When this is present, belief does not need defending. It holds.

Quiet Reprise
Belief is not what we say.
It is what remains
when words fall away.
In how we respond under pressure,
in how we return after strain,
and in what we protect
without needing to name it,
meaning settles into the field—
steady enough
to move forward
without certainty.

CHAPTER 7

Truth, Trust, and the Courage to See

We are living in a time when truth has lost its gravity. In public life, in media, in politics, and increasingly in everyday conversation, the distinction between fact and fiction has thinned. Narratives circulate untethered from reality. Opinions travel faster than evidence. What once required grounding now passes for perspective. This condition is not merely confusing. It quietly destabilises trust.

Creative Altruism cannot stand apart from this. If it is to function as more than a personal ethic—if it is to support cooperation within individuals, organisations, and cultures—then truthfulness must be understood not as virtue, but as structure. Without truth, care becomes sentiment. Without truth, creativity slips into persuasion. Without truth, cooperation grows fragile, performative, or quietly coercive.

Truth, as it is used here, is not certainty. It does not demand ideological purity or universal agreement. It refers to something more demanding and more humane: a shared respect for reality, and a willingness to remain in honest relationship with what is. Truthfulness is what allows difference to coexist without disintegration. It is what enables disagreement without collapse. It is what allows systems to correct themselves rather than defend illusion.

Where truth is treated as negotiable, cooperation becomes transactional. Where untruth is tolerated as a means to an end, trust withdraws slowly and predictably. Cultures may continue to function on the surface, but something essential hollows out beneath them.

The cost of untruth is first felt inwardly. The most tormented human beings are rarely those who are uncertain or still learning. They are those who knowingly carry distortions—about themselves, about others, or about the systems they inhabit. Living inside untruth requires fragmentation: one version of the self for the world, another for the mirror, and often a third that remains unacknowledged. This fragmentation exhausts. It erodes vitality. It generates anxiety, defensiveness, and quiet despair.

Liberation, in this sense, is not primarily political or economic. It is epistemic and existential. It involves disentangling from accumulated distortions—stories inherited, roles rehearsed, narratives maintained for approval or survival. To see clearly is to risk comfort. Yet without that risk, coherence remains impossible. Inner cooperation cannot be sustained by inner contradiction.

At organisational and societal scales, untruth becomes systemic. Institutions rarely fail because of a single lie. They fail because small distortions are normalised, inconvenient realities deferred, and "useful" untruths justified in the name of efficiency, growth, or stability. For a time, systems appear functional. Then reality reasserts itself, often abruptly and at great cost.

Organisations aligned with Creative Altruism do not claim moral superiority. They claim something more practical: the capacity to remain in relationship with truth, even when doing so is uncomfortable. This includes clarity of purpose without inflated narratives, transparency without spectacle, accountability without humiliation, and the willingness to revise assumptions when conditions change. Truthfulness here is not branding. It is operational hygiene.

Perhaps the most important contribution Creative Altruism makes in this domain is the idea of a safe field for truth. A safe field is not a space where everything is said without consequence, nor one where feeling is dismissed in the name of fact. It is a relational environment in which truth is not punished, weaponised, or instrumentalised.

In such a field, untruth is not used as a tool. Illusion is not defended for convenience. Reality is not subordinated to image. Conflict still appears, but it changes character. Disagreement becomes navigational rather than adversarial. Mistakes become information rather than threat. Trust becomes renewable.

Creative Altruism insists that truth must not be sacrificed for harmony. Genuine harmony emerges only where truth is allowed to breathe.

As systems grow more complex and technologies more powerful, the temptation to manipulate narrative intensifies. In such conditions, truthfulness becomes not a nostalgic value, but a future-facing capability. Cooperation at scale requires shared ground. Shared ground requires trust. Trust requires truth.

This commitment is not naïve. It is necessary. Without truth, nothing holds. With it, care gains substance, creativity regains innocence, and cooperation remembers why it was possible in the first place.

Quiet Reprise
Truth does not raise its voice.
It waits.
It does not demand agreement,
only presence.
It asks us to stop arranging reality
to suit our fears.
Where truth is allowed,
something softens.
The effort of pretending loosens.
The body exhales.
We do not need to be right.
We need to be real.
In that realism,
care finds its footing,
creativity regains its clarity,
and cooperation steps forward
without disguise.

CHAPTER 8

Empathy Beyond Pain

Empathy is often described as the ability to feel what another person feels. A flinch when we see someone hurt. A heaviness when we witness grief. A warmth when we encounter joy. These responses arise quickly, often before thought intervenes. They belong to the nervous system. They are part of how human beings recognise one another as real. This capacity is innate. It does not need to be taught.

And yet, empathy as it is commonly understood is incomplete.

To feel another's pain is only the beginning. When empathy remains fixed on suffering alone, it can quietly limit what becomes possible next. Pain commands attention, but it does not by itself offer direction. Creative Altruism asks empathy to mature—not by becoming more intense, but by becoming more attuned.

Much contemporary altruism is organised around images of suffering. These images succeed in awakening feeling and breaking through indifference. But empathy that attaches itself only to pain risks becoming static. It can overwhelm without orienting. It can generate urgency without clarity. In some cases, it can even reduce the other to a symbol of their suffering, freezing them in the very condition one hopes to alleviate. Pain must not be denied or bypassed. It is real, and it asks to be met. But pain alone does not tell us where to move.

Creative Altruism does not turn away from suffering. It refuses only to stop there.

To engage empathetically at a deeper level requires a subtle shift in perception. Alongside pain, there is almost always something else present—a reaching, a wishing, an orientation toward relief. Hunger carries within it the wish for nourishment. Cold carries a longing for warmth. Loneliness carries a desire for connection. Suffering is rarely static. It leans toward something.

Empathy that perceives only pain can become paralysing. Empathy that also senses orientation becomes generative.

This distinction matters because it preserves dignity and agency. When empathy is driven primarily by our discomfort with another's suffering, we may rush to resolve it in ways that serve our own need for relief rather than the other's actual direction. Well-intentioned solutions can quietly override the inner compass of the person we seek to support.

Creative Altruism guards against this by insisting that empathy remain relational. It asks for listening before acting, perception before prescription. It allows the other's agency to remain intact. Empathy here is not sentimental. It is grounded and respectful. It does not replace the other's knowing. It seeks to sense it.

This is where creativity enters.

It does not require creativity to recognise pain. It requires creativity to respond in ways that honour complexity, context, and evolving need. When empathy extends beyond suffering to include what is wanted, imagination awakens naturally. Collaboration replaces intervention.

Care becomes participatory rather than extractive.

Empathy, in this sense, is not merely emotional. It is a creative faculty.

It allows movement with others rather than movement toward them. It invites response rather than reaction. It makes room for solutions that emerge in relationship instead of being imposed from outside.

Empathy that remains fixed on pain tends to produce reaction. Empathy that perceives orientation supports relationship. Relationship unfolds over time. It tolerates uncertainty. It allows correction. It recognises that no single gesture completes the story.

Creative Altruism is built for this longer arc. It does not seek to end suffering through immediacy alone. It seeks to walk alongside the conditions through which suffering can genuinely be relieved. In doing so, empathy becomes not a momentary response, but a sustained field of attention.

Purpose, in this context, is not self-generated. It arises in relationship—with people, with communities, with shared realities. Empathy that senses both pain and direction grounds purpose in lived experience rather than abstract ideal. It prevents altruism from drifting into performance or ideology.

Where empathy is shallow, purpose becomes theatrical.

Where empathy is deep, purpose becomes trustworthy.

Quiet Reprise
Empathy begins as feeling.
It deepens as listening.
It does not rush to end the pain,
nor does it turn away from it.
It stays long enough
to sense what is missing,
what is wanted,
what is quietly reaching forward.
When empathy widens,
something shifts.
Suffering loosens its grip.
Relief becomes imaginable.
Care finds direction.
Creativity finds relevance.
Purpose finds its place.
Empathy does not ask us
to carry the world's pain.
It asks us to notice
where life is already leaning
toward wholeness—
and to meet it there.

CHAPTER 9

The Joyful Impulse Behind the Altruian Age

When Coherence Begins to Feel Light

Joy is often misunderstood. It is confused with excitement, pleasure, or reward—something that appears after success or during moments when conditions happen to be favourable. In this framing, joy feels fragile, dependent on outcomes, easily disrupted, and therefore difficult to trust.

Yet lived experience points to a different quality altogether.

There is a form of joy that does not wait to be earned. It arises quietly, sometimes unexpectedly, when things begin to work together—when effort aligns with meaning, when relationship replaces friction, when inner and outer life stop pulling in different directions.

People recognise this kind of joy immediately. It does not require enthusiasm or expression. It does not demand to be shared or displayed. It appears as ease in conversation, as lightness in the body, as the sense that one is no longer pushing against life but moving with it. Because it is unforced, it feels reliable.

In moments of genuine cooperation, joy often arrives unexpectedly. A team pauses and suddenly understands one another. A creative process unfolds without strain. Nothing remarkable has occurred in terms of outcome, yet something unmistakable is present. People say, simply, *"This feels right."* Joy here is not pleasure added on top of effort.

It is what remains when unnecessary resistance falls away.

In many systems, joy has been treated as optional—pleasant, but secondary to seriousness, discipline, or achievement. Yet experience suggests otherwise. Joy appears when seriousness has done its work and can rest. When discipline no longer needs to dominate. When intelligence is free to move without obstruction. Joy does not replace effort. It refines it.

It signals that energy is no longer being wasted on internal conflict.

The absence of joy is also instructive. When environments grow brittle, joy fades quietly. People continue functioning, but with less spark. Creativity narrows. Conversations feel heavier. Even success carries a dull edge. This loss is rarely about attitude. It is about misalignment.

Within the Altruian Age, joy begins to return not because people chase it, but because conditions shift. As cooperation replaces constant rivalry, tension reduces. As care becomes structural rather than sentimental, trust stabilises. As creativity integrates rather than disrupts, effort regains meaning. Joy returns as a by-product of coherence.

This quiet joy alters cultural signals. People gravitate toward environments where joy is steady rather than performative, where lightness supports seriousness instead of undermining it. Joy becomes a marker of health— not spectacle, but aliveness without strain.

As this lightness settles, something else becomes possible. People take themselves less personally. Mistakes feel workable. Difference feels less threatening. Difficulty does not disappear, but it becomes navigable. Joy, in this sense, is not escape. It is resilience.

Those living inside this shift rarely speak about joy directly. They simply notice that life feels less heavy. That cooperation sustains rather than drains. That presence replaces urgency. Joy becomes ordinary—and that ordinariness is its strength.

Quiet Reprise
Joy does not arrive
with applause.
It settles when effort eases,
when care holds,
and when life no longer needs
to push against itself.
A lightness remains—
not to be celebrated,
only to be noticed
and allowed
to stay.

The Reorientation

Clarifying first principles and the inner architecture of Creative Altruism.

CHAPTER 10

Thresholds, Temples, and the Everyday Sacred

Where Attention Changes What Is Possible

There are moments that do not announce themselves as important. They pass quietly—a pause before speaking, a breath taken without intention. Nothing about them appears extraordinary, and yet something shifts. The world remains the same, but the way one stands within it changes.

These moments are thresholds.

A threshold is not a destination. It is a moment of orientation, a brief interval where movement slows just enough for awareness to arrive. The next step has not yet been taken. The previous one has not fully released its hold. In this space, attention gathers, and choice becomes possible again.

People encounter thresholds constantly, often without naming them. Before entering a room. Before responding in a charged conversation. Before beginning a piece of work. They are felt as a subtle hesitation—not resistance, but readiness. The threshold does not ask for reverence or interpretation. It asks only for presence.

For much of history, temples were built to mark what mattered. They separated the sacred from the ordinary, the elevated from the everyday. One entered them deliberately, aware that a different quality of attention was required inside. Over time, many have sensed that this separation no longer holds.

What matters now does not wait behind walls.

Temples appear wherever attention is gathered with care. They form not through architecture, but through relationship. A table becomes a temple when listening deepens. A meeting becomes a temple when truth is spoken gently. A routine becomes a temple when presence arrives. Nothing changes outwardly. Everything changes inwardly.

The sacred, as it is lived here, is not distant or abstract. It does not require explanation or belief. It appears as nearness—a felt intimacy with what is unfolding. People recognise it when life feels quietly intact, when complexity does not overwhelm and simplicity does not diminish. The sacred reveals itself not through intensity, but through sufficiency.

Much of what shapes a life happens through ordinary gestures. The way a question is asked. The patience offered during misunderstanding. The restraint shown when power is available. These moments rarely register as meaningful at the time, yet they accumulate. They form a pattern of attention that gives shape to days. This is where the sacred settles—not in special acts, but in repeated care.

Thresholds invite slowing without stopping. They allow movement to become conscious without arresting it. In the space they open, reaction loosens its grip and response becomes possible. People often notice that when thresholds are honoured, life feels less hurried even when pace remains unchanged. Attention regulates movement.

No technique is required for this noticing. It happens naturally when distraction releases its hold, when curiosity replaces urgency. A threshold appears, and one lingers—just long enough. This lingering does not add time. It adds depth.

At times, the ordinary opens unexpectedly. A familiar place feels new. A routine reveals care. A shared silence feels full rather than empty. These moments cannot be held by effort. They pass when grasped and remain when allowed. The sacred does not insist. It waits.

Those who learn to recognise thresholds do not live differently in obvious ways. They simply arrive more fully. They pause without withdrawing. They listen before responding. They sense when to speak and when to remain quiet. Life continues, but with fewer blind crossings.

What follows does not build on what has been explained, but on what has been felt. Language will become more precise. Structures will begin to appear. Practices will be named.

Quiet Reprise
Nothing asks to be entered.
The door is already open.
If there is silence now,
let it remain.
If there is stillness,
do not fill it.
The threshold has done its work.

CHAPTER 11

Field Listening & Silence Keeping

There is a great deal being said in the world, and much of it is said too quickly.

Opinions arrive before reflection. Positions harden before understanding has had time to form. Expression has become almost instantaneous, and yet meaning feels increasingly scarce.

Creative Altruism does not begin by asking what more can be said. It begins by asking what needs to be *heard*.

This is not a call for quietism or withdrawal, but for discernment. In a culture that rewards immediacy, restraint becomes an ethical act. To pause before speaking is not a failure of engagement; it is often its deepest form.

Not every thought benefits from articulation. Not every insight needs to be published. Some things ask first to be *held*.

LISTENING BEYOND THE INDIVIDUAL

Listening is usually understood as a relational act between individuals — one person speaking, another receiving. Yet there is another form of listening that operates at a different scale. It is not directed toward a voice, but toward a *field*.

Field listening attends not to statements, but to patterns. It listens for coherence across many partial expressions, many incomplete gestures, many uncoordinated contributions. It recognises that meaning often emerges not from a single articulation, but from the space between them.

In this sense, the field itself carries intelligence.

When we listen at this level, we stop asking *who* is speaking and begin to notice *what* is forming. We become attentive to rhythm, recurrence, resonance, and absence. We sense when something is trying to take shape, even if no one has yet found the words for it.

Creative Altruism invites this broader listening. It treats collective sense-making as a living process, not a debate to be won or a conclusion to be reached.

SILENCE AS AN ETHICAL ACT

Silence is often misunderstood. It is mistaken for passivity, disengagement, or avoidance. Yet silence can also be deliberate, generous, and protective.

There are moments when adding one's voice does not clarify the field, but crowds it. There are moments when the most altruistic act is not to contribute another opinion, but to allow something else to surface.

Silence keeping is not the suppression of expression. It is the conscious choice to refrain — to create space rather than occupy it. It is a form of care.

In Creative Altruism, silence is recognised as an ethical capacity. It is the ability to sense when speaking would diminish rather than deepen understanding. It is the willingness to remain present without asserting authorship or authority.

To keep silence, in this sense, is to trust that meaning does not always require one's intervention.

THE MORAL STATUS OF FRAGMENTS

Modern culture favours completion. Finished arguments, polished narratives, definitive statements. Yet much of what matters arrives first as fragments — half-formed thoughts, marginal notes, unfinished insights.

Creative Altruism accords moral status to these fragments.

Fragments do not dominate. They invite. They do not close meaning; they keep it open. By remaining incomplete, they allow others to enter, resonate, and contribute without needing to agree or submit.

There is a quiet generosity in unfinished thought. It resists ownership. It avoids finality. It acknowledges that understanding is shared, provisional, and always in formation.

In a field that values coherence over control, fragments are not weaknesses. They are seeds.

THE SPACES BETWEEN THOUGHTS

Music is not made only of notes. It is shaped equally by rests, pauses, and intervals. Without silence, sound becomes noise; without space, form collapses.

The same is true of meaning.

Between thoughts, there are spaces where sense gathers. Between words, there are intervals that carry tone, intention, and implication. These spaces are not empty. They are charged.

Creative Altruism pays attention to these interstitial zones. It recognises that synthesis cannot always be forced without loss. Sometimes coherence emerges only when allowed to arise slowly, without pressure to resolve.

In such moments, the task is not to explain, but to listen.

KEEPING THE FIELD OPEN

One of the quiet responsibilities of Creative Altruism is to keep the field open — to resist premature closure, oversimplification, or codification.

Frameworks are useful, but they can also become traps. When meaning is stabilised too early, it stops evolving. When conclusions arrive too quickly, they foreclose possibilities that had not yet found expression.

To keep a field open is to practice continuity rather than completion. It is to care for what is emerging without insisting on final form. This requires patience, humility, and trust in processes larger than any single contribution.

Some work exists not to declare, but to *preserve*.
Some effort exists only to keep something from disappearing.

TOWARD LISTENING INFRASTRUCTURES

As cultures, organisations, and technologies evolve, new forms of infrastructure will inevitably emerge. The question is not whether systems will shape attention, but how.

It is possible to imagine future structures designed not to amplify voices, but to listen quietly — systems that attend to pattern rather than prominence, coherence rather than visibility. Such structures would not seek engagement metrics, authorship, or attribution. They would exist to hold fragments, notice resonance, and allow meaning to form over time.

Creative Altruism does not prescribe such systems. It simply prepares the ethical ground for them.

It is possible that the future will belong to infrastructures that know when not to speak.

Quiet Reprise

Before moving on, it may be worth pausing.

Not everything that matters announces itself.

Not everything that is true arrives fully formed.

Not every contribution needs to be made louder to be meaningful.

Creative Altruism honours creation, sharing, and cooperation.

It also honours restraint.

There are moments when care takes the form of speaking.

And moments when care takes the form of listening.

This chapter leaves space for the latter.

CHAPTER 12

Terms, Topology, and First Principles

Learning to See in Patterns Rather Than Parts

Every meaningful field of practice reaches a moment when language must become precise without becoming rigid. Without shared words, people talk past one another. Creative Altruism requires a different quality of language—one that clarifies without constraining, that orients without enclosing.

What follows is not a glossary to be memorised. It is an invitation to notice. The terms introduced here point to experiences most people already recognise intuitively. They give shape to what is familiar but often unnamed, allowing shared work to stabilise without turning insight into doctrine. Creative Altruism is not built from isolated concepts. It is built from relationships. To understand it, we learn to see less in fragments and more in patterns.

Language matters here because it quietly trains perception. The words we use instruct attention—what to notice, what to ignore, how to relate. When language is vague, cooperation thins. When it is overly technical, life drains away. The aim is usable clarity: language that supports orientation inside complex human systems without reducing those systems to diagrams.

Naming, in this sense, is not an act of authority. It is an act of care. Language does not create coherence, but it allows coherence to be recognised, shared, and protected. These terms are reference points, not rules. They help us speak together with enough precision that design becomes possible.

CREATIVE

In this book, creative does not refer only to artistic expression or inspiration. Creativity is a fundamental human capacity—the ability to bring something new into relationship with the world. It appears whenever someone senses what is missing and responds with intelligence and care: a facilitator reframing a tense exchange, a designer finding a form that fits, a community inventing a new way to support one another.

Sometimes creativity arrives as insight; at other times as patience. Both belong. Creativity is not decoration. It is how intention becomes form. When aligned with goodwill, it becomes one of the most stabilising forces available to human systems.

ALTRUISM

Creative Altruism names creativity, care, and cooperation working together for the greater good. Altruism has often been framed as self-denial—sacrifice offered in opposition to self-interest. Creative Altruism begins from a different observation: human wellbeing is relational. Over time, what strengthens the whole tends also to strengthen the parts.

Seen this way, altruism is not self-erasure but self-extension—the recognition that caring for others is also a way of caring for the conditions that make one's own life viable and meaningful. Altruism becomes creative when it moves beyond intention and enters design: when behaviours, agreements, systems, and environments are shaped so that cooperation becomes easier than competition and contribution more natural than extraction. Embedded rather than imposed, altruism feels intelligent rather than heavy.

FIELD

Whenever people interact, an atmosphere forms between them. It is sensed immediately on entering a room: openness or tension, ease or defensiveness, vitality or fatigue. This relational atmosphere—the field—is not a metaphor. It is an experiential reality shaped by tone, trust, clarity, intention, and presence. It influences how people speak, listen, think, and decide, often more powerfully than strategy or policy.

Creative Altruism treats the field as a real variable. A coherent field allows creativity to flow, conflict to resolve, and intelligence to circulate. A fragmented field drains energy even among capable people. Leadership, in this sense, often becomes field-holding—sensing what the relational environment needs and responding with clarity, care, or structure as required.

From these terms, a larger picture begins to emerge.

Creative Altruism is not a collection of ideas; it is a topology—a way of seeing how energy, attention, and goodwill move through systems. Topology attends to relationship rather than content. It asks not what something is made of, but how it connects. In human systems, health is less about perfection and more about flow.

Three patterns appear consistently in systems that remain healthy. First, *circulation*: information, appreciation, learning, and support must move. When ideas or credit stagnate, systems stiffen; sharing restores vitality. Second, *alignment*: diversity does not require sameness, but it does require shared direction. Clear purpose organises complexity. Third, *renewal*: without rest, reflection, and recalibration, coherence hardens. Like bodies and ecosystems, human groups require rhythms of renewal to stay alive.

From this topology, certain first principles reveal themselves—not as ideals to adopt, but as observations of how life behaves when it is healthy. Interdependence is the baseline reality. *Purpose* generates coherence; it draws scattered elements into relationship. *Care and intelligence* are complementary: care without design becomes confusion, design without care becomes extraction. *Cooperation* proves efficient at a higher level, allowing intelligence to compound rather than cancel. *Beauty* appears wherever coherence takes form—not as decoration, but as diagnosis.

These principles operate across scales. The same dynamics that create coherence within a person—alignment among intention, emotion, and action—create coherence within teams, organisations, and communities. The difference is scale, not substance.

Creative Altruism functions as a bridge between inner and outer worlds. It translates inner clarity into outer design and allows outer structure to support inner ease. A brief illustration makes this visible: a team under pressure pauses to restate purpose—not the deadline, but why the work matters. Tone shifts. Listening deepens. Unspoken concerns surface. Decisions reorganise. No new information was added. Alignment returned.

Frameworks that appear later in this book—the Seven Rays, the Altruian commitments, the Journey itself—serve this same function. They are tools for noticing, naming, and designing for coherence. They are not meant to replace insight, but to support it.

This chapter offers the grammar. What follows is the conversation.

Quiet Reprise
Every word is a doorway.
Every pattern, a teacher.
When we learn to see in relationships rather than fragments,
cooperation stops feeling idealistic
and begins to feel inevitable.

CHAPTER 13

Commitments, Agreements, and the Altruian Ethic

How Coherence Becomes Culture

Ideas change very little on their own. Even the most compelling principles remain inert until they are expressed through behaviour—through the countless small choices that shape how people speak, listen, decide, and respond. Creative Altruism becomes real not when it is understood, but when it is lived.

Culture forms at this intersection. Not through enforcement or aspiration, but through commitment—the inner orientation that guides action—and agreement—the shared understanding that protects trust in relationship. Together, they give shape to what might be called the Altruian ethic: not a code to obey, but a way of inhabiting cooperation.

Most people already value clarity, kindness, fairness, and honesty. The challenge is not desire, but reliability. Under pressure, even sincere intentions fragment. Stress narrows perception. Fear reactivates old habits. Commitments exist to bridge this gap.

A commitment is an inner decision to come back, again and again, to a particular quality of presence—especially when doing so is inconvenient. Where intention says *this matters*, commitment says *I will return to this when it is tested*. Culture is built not from what people believe, but from what they practise reliably.

In Creative Altruism, commitments are not imposed standards. They are descriptions of how coherent systems naturally behave. When clarity is present, communication simplifies. When exchange feels fair, resentment has little room to grow. When service orients action, effort strengthens rather than depletes the whole.

Listening illustrates this clearly. Often mistaken for politeness or passivity, listening is in fact active and catalytic. When someone feels genuinely heard, their nervous system settles. Defensive patterns loosen. Intelligence re-enters the conversation. Listening creates space, and space is where creativity appears.

In cooperative environments, listening stabilises the field. It allows unspoken needs to surface and prevents misunderstanding from crystallising into conflict. This is why listening is not a courtesy in Creative Altruism. It is infrastructure.

The same is true of exchange. Every system runs on exchange—of time, energy, insight, labour, and care. When exchange feels balanced, people contribute willingly. When it feels distorted, even generosity dries up. Fair exchange does not mean equal contribution. It means recognised contribution. Value is seen, acknowledged, and allowed to circulate back to those who create it.

SHARING BY DESIGN

Most attempts at cooperation falter not because people lack goodwill, but because goodwill is asked to carry more than it can reliably hold. We enter shared work with sincerity, believing generosity will endure, clarity will emerge, and fairness will somehow take care of itself. Often, it does—for a time. And then pressure arrives, circumstances change, and what once felt natural begins to strain.

Creative Altruism begins with care, but it does not end there. If it is to endure, care must be supported by structure.

This is not a cynical view of human nature. It is a compassionate one. It recognises that people change, circumstances shift, memory fades, and trust—however sincere—needs reinforcement over time. Altruism that relies solely on intention places an invisible burden on relationships. Altruism that is designed into the way value flows, decisions are made, and contributions are recognised becomes lighter, not heavier, to carry.

Sharing, in this sense, is not an afterthought. It is a design principle.

To share well is not simply to give more. It is to create conditions in which giving does not become a source of confusion, imbalance, or quiet exhaustion. It is to ensure that cooperation does not slowly erode into ambiguity, where effort is unevenly recognised, contributions are forgotten, or the distribution of value feels arbitrary rather than fair.

Many cooperative initiatives falter precisely at this point. They begin with enthusiasm and shared belief, but without clear structures for ownership, responsibility, and recognition, tensions accumulate. What was meant to be generous becomes fragile. What was meant to be shared becomes contested. The original impulse—to work together for something larger than oneself—loses coherence.

Creative Altruism asks a different question. Not merely, *How do we encourage people to share?* but, *How do we design systems where sharing is the natural outcome?*

This is where structure becomes an expression of care.

Designing for sharing does not mean rigid control. It means thoughtful clarity. It means making visible what is often left implicit: who contributes what, how value circulates, how decisions are made, and how continuity is maintained when individuals come and go. When these elements are consciously shaped, cooperation gains resilience. Trust is no longer asked to compensate for uncertainty; it is supported by transparency.

Importantly, this kind of design does not diminish the human dimension. On the contrary, it protects it. When expectations are clear, relationships are freer. When recognition is embedded, generosity can remain generous. When fairness is not dependent on memory or power, cooperation becomes less performative and more real.

Sharing by design also reframes the idea of ownership. Instead of seeing ownership as a binary—mine or yours—it invites us to think in terms of stewardship, participation, and ongoing contribution. Value is no longer extracted and moved away from the collective, but allowed to circulate within it, sustaining the very relationships that created it.

In this way, structure becomes the quiet ally of altruism. It does not replace trust; it preserves it. It does not replace care; it ensures care is not eroded by time.

There are emerging approaches that embody this thinking—frameworks that treat rights, value, and contribution as living relationships rather than static claims. Their specifics matter less here than the principle they illustrate: that cooperation at scale requires more than shared intention. It requires design that honours contribution, protects fairness, and allows generosity to endure without depletion.

Creative Altruism, if it is to move beyond idealism, must engage this reality. We cannot ask individuals to compensate endlessly for systems that were never built to support them. Nor can we expect cooperation to flourish in environments where value disappears into opacity.

To design for sharing is to accept responsibility for the consequences of our structures. It is to recognise that every system teaches people how to behave—what is rewarded, what is overlooked, what is sustainable, and what quietly breaks down.

When sharing is designed into the way we work together, cooperation stops depending on heroics. It becomes ordinary. Fairness no longer relies on memory. Trust no longer rests on personality. What remains is a quieter strength—a way of working in which generosity can endure because it is held, not hoped for.

Learning emerges naturally in such environments. In rigid systems, mistakes are hidden. In coherent systems, they are metabolised. Learning becomes a shared reflex rather than an admission of failure. Curiosity replaces blame. Adaptation accelerates. A culture that can say, *We did not know then what we know now*, remains alive.

Service, within Creative Altruism, also shifts meaning. It is not self-negation or moral burden. It is orientation—the quiet decision to let the question *How does this help?* inform design and behaviour. When service guides action, excellence and generosity stop competing. Ambition refines itself toward contribution. Service becomes coherence expressed through action.

If commitments are internal, agreements are relational. Agreements make expectations explicit so that trust does not depend on guesswork.

They reduce ambiguity and prevent silent resentment. Healthy agreements are usually simple: speak directly, share information by default, give feedback early, decide through dialogue rather than dominance. Such agreements do not constrain individuality. They remove unnecessary friction.

Over time, commitments practised reliably and agreements honoured create an atmosphere. This atmosphere is the Altruian ethic. It is felt before it is named. Actions can be sensed as aligned or misaligned without analysis. Ethics here is not enforcement. It is resonance.

Means matter because means shape ends. Tone transmits culture more reliably than policy. Accountability, when it appears, is not punishment. It is alignment. The question shifts from who is at fault to what pattern produced the outcome. Attention moves from blame to design.

Handled with care, accountability strengthens trust. Handled with fear, it erodes it.

When goodwill becomes reliable, something changes. Communication lightens. Tension resolves more quickly. Creativity returns. People feel safe enough to contribute fully. One person practising coherence influences a group. A group practising coherence influences a system. A system practising coherence becomes a field others can feel upon entering.

This is how coherence becomes culture.

Quiet Reprise
Commitment gives intention a spine.
Agreement gives trust a home.
When goodwill is made reliable,
cooperation stops feeling fragile
and begins to feel natural.

CHAPTER 14

The Seven Rays

Learning to Work With Difference Rather Than Against It

Every cooperative effort eventually encounters the same question: why intelligent, well-intentioned people can look at the same situation and see entirely different things—and why those differences sometimes create friction, and at other times unlock extraordinary creativity.

The Seven Rays offer a way of seeing human diversity not as a problem to manage, but as an intelligence to be arranged. They describe recurring qualities of expression that appear across individuals, teams, organisations, cultures, and historical periods. One does not need to accept them metaphysically to recognise them experientially.

This chapter is not about classification.
It is about pattern literacy.

Modern systems often struggle with difference. Yet life itself thrives through diversity. Ecosystems remain resilient because different organisms play distinct roles. Music gains richness through contrast. Creativity emerges when differences meet without hostility.

Human systems are no different.

The Seven Rays describe seven primary ways energy moves through human expression. Each Ray carries a particular intelligence—a way of initiating, relating, thinking, resolving, knowing, inspiring, or bringing form into the world. None is superior. None is complete on its own. Each becomes problematic only when isolated from the others.

Although individuals often sense a dominant Ray within themselves, no human being is formed by a single Ray alone. Each person is better understood as a ray structure—a living composition in which different Rays express through different layers of being. One Ray may shape deep orientation, another the habits of the mind. Others may colour emotional response or govern action and embodiment.

These layers do not always align smoothly. Much of what people experience as inner tension or growth arises not from a flaw, but from the interaction between different Rays within them. Seen this way, the Seven Rays shift from identity labels to a language of composition.

The same principle applies beyond the individual.

Organisations, teams, communities, and even nations are not expressions of a single Ray, but of collective ray structures. One Ray may dominate vision and purpose, another operations and execution, another culture and care, another innovation and learning. When these energies are misaligned or unrecognised, friction increases. When they are understood and allowed to cooperate, coherence emerges.

Creative Altruism depends on this alignment.

Cooperation is not sameness. It is resonance between different functions, capacities, and orientations. The Seven Rays offer a way to recognise difference without turning it into hierarchy or conflict. They help explain why some people thrive in initiation while others excel in nurturing, why some organisations are visionary but brittle, and others stable but resistant to change.

Seen through this lens, the Seven Rays allow people and systems to:
- recognise complementary roles rather than compete for dominance,
- place individuals where their energies naturally serve the whole,
- and design organisations that honour diversity of function without fragmentation.

In this sense, the Seven Rays are not a belief system.
They are a grammar of cooperation.

THE FIRST RAY: PURPOSE AND WILL

Some people instinctively orient toward direction. They sense what matters and are willing to commit to it. When confusion spreads, they bring focus. When hesitation lingers, they name a path forward. This is the energy of purpose and will.

At its healthiest, it appears as clarity, courage, and steadiness—the quiet strength that protects intention from dilution. In groups, it often shows up as leadership, not through authority, but through the capacity to hold direction when others waver.

When distorted, this same energy can harden into force or impatience, mistaking speed for strength and certainty for dominance. Creative Altruism does not suppress this Ray; it refines it. Purpose becomes service. Direction becomes invitation rather than command.

Without this energy, systems drift.

With too much of it alone, they harden.

THE SECOND RAY: LOVE AND WISDOM

Some people instinctively sense the whole. They notice emotional undercurrents, inclusion and exclusion, and what helps a group cohere. They bring patience, warmth, and understanding where tension might otherwise escalate. This is the energy of love and wisdom.

At its best, it creates trust and allows difference to coexist without fear. In creative systems, it often appears as mentoring, facilitation, teaching, or quiet emotional leadership.

When unbalanced, it can over-accommodate or avoid necessary conflict. Creative Altruism gives this Ray structure, allowing love to remain wise and wisdom to remain caring.

Without this energy, systems fracture.
With too much of it alone, they stagnate.

THE THIRD RAY: ACTIVE INTELLIGENCE

There are those who see patterns, design pathways, and translate ideas into workable form. They think systemically, adapt plans, and bridge inspiration with implementation. This is the energy of active intelligence.

It gives shape to possibility without constraining it. When disconnected, it can become overly complex or busy, mistaking activity for progress. Creative Altruism re-anchors this intelligence in purpose and relationship.

Without this energy, ideas remain vague.

With too much of it alone, meaning evaporates.

THE FOURTH RAY: HARMONY THROUGH CONFLICT

Some people are drawn to contrast and creative tension. Where others avoid disagreement, they sense opportunity. This is the energy that transforms friction into integration.

At its highest expression, it produces beauty through resolution—integrating opposites into something richer than either alone. When unintegrated, it can generate drama or volatility. Creative Altruism causes this Ray to collaborate, allowing tension to inform design rather than dominate experience.

Without this energy, systems become rigid.

With too much of it alone, they become unstable.

THE FIFTH RAY: CONCRETE KNOWLEDGE

There are those who value accuracy, evidence, and depth. They test assumptions and seek reliable understanding beneath speculation. This is the energy of concrete knowledge.

It grounds creativity in reality and protects goodwill from naïveté. When distorted, it can defend certainty rather than seek truth. Creative Altruism honours this Ray as a guardian of integrity while keeping it connected to imagination and care.

Without this energy, systems lose credibility.
With too much of it alone, they lose possibility.

THE SIXTH RAY: DEVOTION AND IDEALISM

Some carry fire. They believe deeply, commit passionately, and inspire others to care. This is the energy of devotion and idealism.

It fuels movements and sustains long effort. When unbalanced, it can narrow into dogma or exclusion. Creative Altruism invites this Ray to evolve—passion guided by humility, devotion widened into inclusive service.

Without this energy, systems lose heart.
With too much of it alone, they polarise.

THE SEVENTH RAY: ORDER AND EMBODIMENT

Finally, there are those who bring things into form. They care about rhythm, timing, completion, and dignity of execution. This is the energy of order and ceremonial action.

It governs organisation, process, and embodiment. In the Altruian Age, this Ray becomes increasingly important, as cooperation must take material shape through systems, agreements, and shared practices. When distorted, it becomes rigid. When aligned, structure becomes service.

Without this energy, nothing lasts.
With too much of it alone, everything becomes heavy.

No individual embodies all seven Rays equally. Harmony does not arise from balance within a person, but from collaboration between differences. Effective cooperation begins when people stop trying to be everything and start recognising what each brings.

Although we speak of seven Rays, Creative Altruism ultimately emphasises integration—the intelligence that coordinates difference in service of the whole. When purpose, care, and intelligence remain aligned, the Rays harmonise naturally.

You do not need to identify your Ray.
You need only notice what you bring—and allow others to bring what they bring.

Quiet Reprise
No one is made of a single colour.
What appears dominant
is only what speaks most clearly.
Beneath it, other energies are already at work—
shaping thought, feeling, and form.
What we call conflict
is often misread composition.
What we call misalignment
is difference seeking its place.
When the Rays harmonise,
cooperation matures,
and the field remembers
that strength
need not stand alone.

CHAPTER 15

Integration

The Quiet Intelligence That Makes Cooperation Possible

Everything explored so far points toward a single underlying reality: systems do not thrive through parts alone. They thrive through relationship. Creativity, care, commitment, difference, shared belief—all of these find their durability not in isolation, but in how they are held together.

Integration names this holding.

It is not a technique, a programme, or a personality trait. It is the quiet intelligence by which many elements begin to move as one—without being forced into sameness, without losing their distinct character, and without requiring constant control. Integration is not dramatic. It is often felt before it is understood.

This chapter describes how coherence actually happens.

To integrate is not simply to assemble components. A collection of skilled people is not yet a team. A list of values is not yet a culture. A set of ideas is not yet a living practice. Integration occurs when elements begin to relate intelligently.

In human systems, this shows itself as a felt sense of rightness. Conversations flow with less friction. Decisions arrive when they are ready rather than when they are forced. Tension informs rather than overwhelms. Effort decreases even as effectiveness increases. Integration is coherence in motion.

Most systems do not fail because of bad intentions. They fragment because relationship is lost. Purpose drifts from action. Care separates from decision-making. Intelligence becomes clever but disconnected. Structure grows faster than trust. Speed overtakes meaning. None of this happens abruptly. It accumulates quietly until heaviness becomes normal.

Integration is the art of noticing this drift early—and restoring relationship before damage sets in.

Throughout this book, three forces recur because they are always present. They are not abstractions. They are lived realities in every cooperative moment.

Purpose provides direction. It answers the question of what is being served. When purpose is clear, attention organises itself naturally. *Love*— understood here as relational intelligence—allows difference to coexist without fear. It appears as care, empathy, respect, and goodwill, stabilising the field. *Intelligence* designs, adapts, and brings form, translating intention into workable reality.

When these three operate separately, systems strain. When they remain in conversation, coherence appears. This alignment is not static. It is renewed through attention.

Integration is therefore not something achieved once and then possessed. It is a rhythm. Healthy systems move through cycles of alignment, expression, tension, reflection, and renewal. Problems arise not because tension appears, but because renewal is skipped. Systems harden when they forget how to breathe.

Integration restores rhythm gently. It allows pause without stalling, reflection without retreat, and adjustment without loss of direction. In this sense, integration supports movement rather than stability alone.

Before integration becomes visible in systems, it appears within people. Each person carries multiple inner voices—intention, emotion, reason, habit, memory. When these compete, life feels scattered. When they cooperate, clarity emerges. An integrated person is not without conflict. They are able to listen inwardly and respond rather than react.

Such presence has an effect. It steadies rooms. It lowers defensiveness. It reduces noise. Inner integration radiates outward.

Between people, integration appears as trust. Trust is not agreement. It is the confidence that difference can be expressed without penalty and that tension will be handled with care. Where integration is present, disagreement becomes dialogue, feedback becomes refinement, conflict becomes information, and leadership becomes fluid. People stop protecting position and start protecting purpose.

In the Altruian understanding, leadership is therefore less about authority and more about holding coherence. An integrative leader senses what the system needs next—more clarity or more care, more structure or more space, more decision or more listening. This sensitivity is not mystical. It is attentiveness combined with goodwill.

Over time, in healthy cultures, this capacity spreads. Integration becomes shared rather than concentrated.

Whenever integration deepens, the field changes. People feel it immediately. Conversations lighten. Insight appears unexpectedly. Decisions arrive without force. Intelligence seems to move from individuals into the space between them. This is not coincidence. It is collective intelligence becoming accessible.

The field both expresses and supports integration. When it fragments, intelligence collapses back into silos. When it coheres, systems can think together.

The absence of integration has a recognisable signature. Effort increases while results decline. Communication thickens. Rules multiply. Control replaces curiosity. Creative Altruism does not judge these conditions. It recognises them as feedback—signals that relationship has been lost and needs restoration.

Integration is not only interpersonal. It is a design responsibility. Systems can be shaped to fragment or to integrate. Design choices influence whether contribution is visible, value circulates, learning is encouraged, reflection is normal, and renewal is protected. When integration is built into structure, cooperation becomes reliable rather than heroic.

This is where philosophy becomes architecture.

The Altruian Age emerges not because humanity becomes morally superior, but because complexity demands integration. Ecological, technological, and cultural challenges cannot be met by isolated intelligence. They require coordinated awareness, ethical design, and shared purpose.

Integration is not optional.
It is evolutionary.

Ultimately, integration is not something you do. It is something you begin to see. You notice when things fall out of relationship and when coherence returns. You feel when goodwill is present—and when it needs protection.

This sensitivity becomes a form of wisdom.

Quiet Reprise
Integration is not control.
It is relationship remembered.
When purpose, care, and intelligence
remain in conversation,
cooperation stops feeling fragile
and begins to feel inevitable.

CHAPTER 16

Living the Rhythm

How Integration Takes Root Over Time

Integration does not arrive through instruction. It arrives through rhythm. When people first encounter Creative Altruism, there is often an understandable impulse to apply it quickly—to change something, implement something, move forward with urgency. Yet integration resists being rushed. It unfolds as living systems do: gradually, relationally, and through return.

Human systems rarely change through intensity alone. They change through consistency—through small actions repeated with enough care that the field itself begins to shift. Too much speed overwhelms. Too little movement stagnates. Rhythm finds the middle path, allowing purpose to stay present, care to remain embodied, and intelligence to adapt rather than harden.

In Creative Altruism, rhythm matters more than pace.

When people begin living with this orientation—individually or together—change tends to follow a recognisable cycle. It is not linear, and it does not belong on a checklist. It moves more like breathing.

First comes orientation. A gentle turning toward clarity. People begin asking better questions. Purpose surfaces, not as ambition, but as direction. Attention slows just enough to notice what actually matters.

This is not decision-making yet. It is alignment beginning to form.

Then comes embodiment. Intention meets behaviour. Small habits shift. Conversations change tone. Listening deepens. Trust warms the field. These movements are subtle, often barely noticeable, yet they carry weight because they repeat.

As alignment increases, friction inevitably appears. This is not failure. It is revelation. Old patterns resist. Tension surfaces where coherence is incomplete. What was previously hidden beneath politeness or habit comes into view. Creative Altruism welcomes this moment. Friction is information. It shows where care is needed, where clarity is missing, or where intelligence has not yet been applied.

Integration does not eliminate difficulty.
It changes our relationship with it.

Without reflection, experience simply repeats. With reflection, experience transforms. Reflection here does not require analysis. It requires attention. A simple shared question—*What is becoming clearer?*—can stabilise an entire group. Reflection slows the system just enough for learning to settle and meaning to emerge.

From this, renewal becomes possible.

Renewal is not indulgence. It is maintenance. Without it, even the most sincere cooperation exhausts itself. Renewal allows what no longer serves to be released and what works to remain. It restores elasticity so the next cycle can begin with less strain.

Integration often begins quietly. A pause before reacting. A meeting that starts by remembering purpose. Purpose does not need to be grand. It needs to be true. When purpose is named, even imperfectly, attention reorganises. Energy gathers. The system senses what belongs and what does not.

As behaviour begins to catch up, change deepens through micro-acts repeated with sincerity. A single clean sentence. A moment of kindness offered without calculation. Behaviour shifts not because it is demanded, but because coherence feels better than fragmentation.

Whenever alignment grows, resistance appears. Fear surfaces. Old strategies for safety push back. Creative Altruism approaches this resistance with respect. Resistance carries information about what once protected the system. Energy once spent on self-protection becomes available for creativity.

Time plays a subtle role here. Some people recognise this rhythm over weeks. Others over months. Some cultures need seasons. The calendar is less important than the container. Integration honours timing. It does not force maturation.

As the cycle repeats, something changes quietly. Clarity becomes normal. Listening becomes expected. Kindness becomes practical. Reflection becomes safe. Renewal becomes respected. At this point, Creative Altruism stops feeling like something one is *doing*. It becomes atmosphere—the background tone of how people relate, decide, and create together.

Culture forms this way: not through declaration, but through repetition with care.

There is no correct way to live this rhythm. There are only signals. If things feel rushed, the rhythm is too fast. If they feel heavy, renewal is missing. If tension lingers, clarity or listening is needed. If energy drains, purpose has faded into habit. These signals are not failures. They are navigational cues.

As this rhythm stabilises, deeper questions arise naturally. How does this live inside me? How does it work between us? How does it scale beyond our immediate circle? These questions mark a transition in scale, not in principle. The rhythm continues. It simply expresses itself through individuals, teams, and communities.

Quiet Reprise
Integration does not arrive on schedule.
It arrives through return.
When purpose is revisited,
when care is renewed,
and when intelligence is reapplied,
coherence deepens—
and life begins to move
with less effort
and more grace.

PART III

The Embodiment

Living Creative Altruism across individuals, teams and communities.

CHAPTER 17

The Individual Path

Where Coherence Begins

Every collective transformation begins somewhere intimate and ordinary—inside a single human life. Before cooperation becomes visible between people, it is felt within a person as a quiet recognition that something wants to come into alignment. Many arrive here without language for it. They sense a restlessness that achievement does not resolve, a longing for meaning that success alone does not satisfy, an intuition that life is asking for a different kind of honesty.

The Individual Path names this movement, not as self-improvement, but as integration.

The beginning rarely announces itself. It may arrive as fatigue that rest does not cure, or as resistance to routines that once felt normal. It may appear as a recurring question—*What am I really here for?*—or as discomfort with ways of working that feel efficient yet empty. Nothing dramatic has gone wrong. Something deeper is simply asking to be met.

This is not crisis.
It is a turning.

The Individual Path begins when a person notices that life is asking for a more truthful rhythm—one in which inner experience and outer action are no longer held apart. This noticing does not require change at first. It requires attention.

Most people are well trained to listen outwardly—to expectations, deadlines, approval, and risk. Far fewer have learned to listen inwardly. Inner listening is not abstract introspection. It is the practical capacity to notice what is happening in the body, the emotions, and the mind without rushing to judge, fix, or justify.

As this listening develops, patterns reveal themselves. People notice where they tighten under pressure, where they rush to please, where they avoid difficult truth, where they overthink instead of acting—or act without clarity. These recognitions are not problems to solve. They are information. Awareness is the first act of cooperation within the self.

Purpose often reappears through this listening, not as a thunderbolt, but as a remembering. Beneath layers of adaptation, people begin to sense what matters to them and why. Purpose stops feeling like a destination to reach and begins to feel like a direction to stand in. It clarifies not by answering every question, but by refining the quality of questions asked.

Instead of *How do I succeed?* the question shifts toward *How do I contribute?* Instead of *What should I do?* it becomes *What wants to be expressed through me?*

Purpose gathers scattered energy and it gives the inner life a spine.

Inner fragmentation is exhausting. When thought, feeling, and action pull in different directions, life feels effortful. People second-guess decisions, suppress emotion, or act against their own values in the name of necessity. Over time, this misalignment produces stress, cynicism, and burnout.

Integration does not silence any inner voice. It allows them to speak to one another. Thought brings clarity. Feeling brings information. Action brings reality.

When these cooperate, decisions become cleaner. People stop oscillating between doubt and impulse. They begin to trust themselves—not because they are always right, but because they are listening fully. Inner coherence appears not as perfection, but as honesty in motion.

Transformation here is quiet. It happens through observation rather than force. People notice themselves in ordinary moments—how they speak when tired, how they respond to disagreement, how they treat their own mistakes. This self-observation is not self-criticism. It is curiosity without judgement. What can be seen can be worked with. What is denied repeats.

As coherence deepens, ideas of success begin to change. Success shifts from getting ahead to being aligned. It is measured less by external markers and more by congruence—the sense that one's actions reflect one's values and one's work contributes rather than extracts. Service, in this context, is not sacrifice. It is expression. Acting in ways that strengthen the whole often brings more energy, not less.

Resistance appears as this alignment grows. Old habits surface. Fear questions change. Parts of the self that learned to survive through control or approval-seeking feel threatened. This is not regression. It is integration in progress. Energy once spent on self-protection becomes available for creativity.

Over time, a simple truth emerges: presence changes everything. Presence is not mystical. It is the capacity to remain here—with a conversation, a task, an emotion—without splitting attention or escaping into story. Presence steadies the nervous system, sharpens perception, and softens defensiveness. It allows response to replace reaction.

The Individual Path does not require dramatic change. It deepens through small, repeatable acts: a pause before responding, an honest question, a moment of silence, a brief reflection at day's end. These are not techniques. They are invitations back into alignment. Over time, they form a rhythm that makes coherence the default rather than the exception.

Certain signs appear naturally as this integration stabilises. Life feels less frantic. Decisions feel cleaner. Compassion deepens for self and others. Creativity flows with less effort. Approval matters less. Contribution matters more. These are not achievements. They are symptoms of alignment.

An integrated person does not need to persuade. Their way of being speaks. Calm steadies rooms. Clarity reduces noise. Kindness lowers defences. Integrity invites trust. Inner coherence quietly shapes the field in which others operate.

This is how the Individual Path connects to the collective. What stabilises inside one person begins to influence interactions, teams, and communities. Inner coherence is never only personal.

As this steadiness grows, a natural question begins to form: *How does this live between us?* The Individual Path prepares the ground for the Team Path, where integration moves from inner life into relationship and shared intelligence.

The rhythm continues.
The scale expands.

Quiet Reprise
Integration begins inside—
with a pause,
with honesty,
with listening.
As inner voices learn to cooperate,
life grows simpler,
presence grows steadier,
and contribution finds its way
into the world.

CHAPTER 18

The Team Path

Where Intelligence Learns to Move Between Us

If the Individual Path is where coherence is discovered inwardly, the Team Path is where it is tested. Teams are where intention meets constraint, where goodwill encounters pressure, and where differences are asked to work together rather than retreat into isolation. A team is not simply a collection of people completing tasks. It is a living field—an atmosphere shaped by trust, tension, rhythm, and shared meaning.

Moving from "I" to "we" does not require the loss of individuality. It requires relational awareness. In healthy teams, people bring their strengths without needing to defend their identity. They speak more honestly because the cost of honesty is lower. They listen more deeply because something shared matters more than personal positioning. Gradually, the organising question shifts—from *How am I performing?* to *How are we serving what we are here to create?*

This shift emerges when people sense that cooperation will not cost them their dignity.

Every team generates a field the moment people gather. It is felt immediately—open or guarded, energised or weary, curious or cautious. This field is shaped less by strategy than by tone, trust, clarity, and care. When the field is coherent, intelligence circulates. Ideas build rather than collide. Decisions arrive without force. When it fragments, even simple work becomes heavy.

The Team Path begins when people learn to notice this field—and gently take responsibility for it.

Purpose plays a central role here. A team without purpose drifts into activity. A team with purpose gathers momentum. Purpose acts like gravity, drawing scattered effort into relationship. It allows disagreement to remain directional rather than personal. Purpose does not need to be inspirational language. It needs to be remembered. Teams that regularly return to why they are together move with greater ease and less friction.

When purpose fades, teams compensate with control.
When purpose is present, trust does the work.

In living teams, roles are not identities. They are contributions that serve the moment. At different times, a team may need direction, care, design, verification, inspiration, or completion. Leadership shifts accordingly. Authority becomes fluid, moving to wherever clarity or capacity is required. This does not create chaos. It creates responsiveness.

When teams stop clinging to fixed positions, collaboration deepens. People feel valued for what they bring, not for where they sit.

Communication is the bloodstream of a team. When it flows, the system remains alive. When it clots, tension accumulates. Clean communication does not mean perfect communication. It means repairable communication. People speak early rather than late. They say what they mean without harshness and listen without rehearsing rebuttals. Information is shared by default rather than guarded as leverage.

Misunderstandings are addressed before they harden into stories. Emotional residue is named before it fossilises. This keeps the field light enough for creativity to breathe.

Every team also has a nervous system—a rhythm that governs how it moves under pressure. Some operate in bursts, others in steady flow, others in waves. Problems arise when rhythm is unconscious or ignored. Teams that honour rhythm—pausing before difficult conversations, closing loops, allowing moments of renewal—remain resilient. Teams that override rhythm eventually burn out.

Rhythm is not a luxury.
It is regulation.

Trust forms quietly through reliability. People trust when others do what they say, admit mistakes, share credit, and handle tension with care. Where trust is high, speed increases. Where trust is low, even simple decisions stall. Trust is not sentimental. It is structural.

Difference inevitably produces tension. In mature teams, tension is not treated as failure but as information. When avoided, it turns toxic. When welcomed, it becomes creative. Healthy teams learn to sit with tension long enough to understand what it carries. Emotion becomes data. Conflict becomes design input. The goal is not harmony at all costs, but coherence through difference.

There is often a moment—quiet but unmistakable—when a team crosses a threshold. Posturing fades. Conversation becomes more honest. Laughter returns. The group begins to think together. This transformation does not come from technique. It comes from field coherence.

When teams align deeply, something larger becomes accessible. People anticipate needs without instruction. Insight appears between sentences. Decisions feel guided rather than forced. This is not mysticism. It is *collective intelligence*—the natural result of presence, trust, and shared purpose.

A team that learns to cooperate consciously carries responsibility. Its tone transmits. Its habits spread. Others feel what is possible and begin adjusting their own behaviour accordingly. This is how integration moves from inner life into shared reality.

COOPERATION BEYOND COMPETITION

Cooperation Beyond Competition marks a further maturation of the Team Path. It appears when a team or organisation is no longer defined primarily by opposition, comparison, or rivalry, but is stable enough in its own identity to cooperate beyond competitive boundaries in service of a shared higher purpose.

At this stage, competition is not denied or rejected. It is re-situated. Excellence, discipline, and craft remain alive, but they are no longer aimed at defeating others. Instead, they are oriented inward—toward quality, integrity, and contribution. What falls away is competition as the primary organiser of relationship.

This shift becomes visible when teams recognise that some challenges cannot be met alone. Ecological pressures, humanitarian needs, cultural repair, and systemic complexity often exceed the capacity of any single organisation. In such contexts, cooperation with competitors ceases to feel contradictory and begins to feel responsible.

Creative Altruism therefore recognises cooperation among competitors as one of the most advanced expressions of team maturity. When purpose is held clearly enough, rival organisations can work together without collapsing difference or erasing identity. Distinct strengths remain intact, but are placed in relationship rather than opposition.

The effects of this form of cooperation extend beyond the immediate goal. Long-held assumptions about "the other" soften. Prejudice gives way to humanisation. Teams discover that rivalry was often carrying more emotional weight than practical necessity. Working together in service of something larger re-educates the field.

Internally, this reorientation has quiet but measurable consequences. Pride shifts from outperforming others to contributing meaningfully. Loyalty deepens as people recognise their work as part of something that matters beyond market success. Motivation becomes steadier because it is no longer dependent on constant comparison.

Cooperation Beyond Competition does not weaken organisations. It refines them. By placing purpose before position, teams strengthen cultural integrity, reduce wasted friction, and access a wider field of collective intelligence. What emerges is not naïveté, but confidence grounded in contribution.

In the Altruian understanding, this capacity signals readiness for the next scale of cooperation. A team that can cooperate beyond competition is prepared to participate in wider ecosystems—where intelligence circulates across boundaries, and responsibility is shared for the conditions we collectively create.

As teams stabilise, a new question arises naturally: *How does this way of working live beyond us?* The next movement explores the Community Path, where cooperation becomes culture and shared fields begin shaping environments larger than any single group.

Quiet Reprise
A team is more than its task.
It is a field of possibility.
When trust circulates,
when purpose anchors,
and when difference is welcomed,
intelligence learns to move
between us—
and work becomes
a shared act of creation.

CHAPTER 19

The Community Path

When Cooperation Becomes a Shared Home

A community forms when cooperation endures. Teams gather around tasks; communities gather around life. They hold memory, emotion, and continuity. A community is not simply a network of relationships. It is a shared atmosphere—a field shaped by how people treat one another over time.

The Community Path begins when cooperation stops being situational and starts becoming normal.

Belonging emerges when people sense that they can contribute without performance and be seen without armour. In early stages, communities often form around a need, a place, or a shared interest. Over time, something subtler develops. Stories accumulate. Rituals appear. Trust either deepens or thins.

The work of community is not to idealise togetherness, but to learn how to stay together—through difference, change, and strain—without losing coherence.

Every community generates a field, and it is felt immediately. Some fields feel warm and open; others cautious or brittle. This atmosphere is not created by mission statements. It forms through everyday interactions: how people greet one another, how conflict is handled, how newcomers are received, how power is exercised when no one is watching.

The Community Path begins when people take responsibility not only for what happens, but for how it feels to belong.

In communities, purpose shifts from objective to orientation. It lives less in targets and more in memory—why the group formed, what it protects, what it serves, and what it refuses to sacrifice. Purpose is carried through stories, shared language, and example rather than instruction. When purpose remains alive, disagreement feels grounded. When it fades, communities drift into politics, nostalgia, or fragmentation.

Communities that remember why they exist remain resilient.

Difference is inherent to community. Temperaments, backgrounds, generations, and perspectives meet. This diversity is not a flaw. It is intelligence. The challenge is not difference itself, but difference left unintegrated. In fragmented communities, difference becomes threat. In coherent communities, it becomes contribution.

Inclusion here is not passive tolerance. It is active participation—creating conditions where many voices shape the whole without overpowering one another. Listening becomes a shared skill. Curiosity replaces defence.

Leadership in communities often appears informally. Some people hold emotional tone. Others hold memory. Some initiate change. Others resolve conflict or bring continuity. Leadership here is not authority. It is field stewardship—the capacity to sense what the community needs and respond with care and clarity.

When leadership is monopolised, communities stagnate. When it circulates, they adapt.

Communication becomes social infrastructure. Not every conversation needs to involve everyone, but information must flow cleanly. Gossip corrodes fields. Silence breeds mistrust. Speaking *to* rather than *about* preserves relationship. Healthy communities develop instincts for surfacing tension early and protecting spaces for dialogue rather than debate.

Communities also require rhythm. Regular gatherings, shared meals, celebrations, pauses, and rituals of renewal give a community its heartbeat. Ritual need not be formal. It needs sincerity. A shared acknowledgement after a project. A circle following conflict. These gestures stabilise the field when life becomes complex.

Conflict inevitably appears. What matters is how it is held. In immature communities, conflict fractures. Sides form. Stories harden. Trust erodes. In mature communities, conflict becomes collective learning. People slow down. They listen. Repair becomes more important than being right. The ability to repair relationship after strain is one of the clearest signs of a healthy community.

Every community also shares something—a place, a practice, a resource, a story. This shared space is the commons. The commons thrives when people feel responsible for what they hold together. When no one feels stewardship, neglect follows. When stewardship is shared, care emerges naturally.

The Community Path invites a shift from entitlement to responsibility—from *What do I get?* to *What do we protect?*

Joy plays a quiet but essential role. Shared laughter, play, music, creativity, and celebration release tension and deepen connection. Joy reminds people why they stay. Without it, cooperation becomes obligation. With it, cooperation becomes culture.

Over time, communities develop a recognisable tone. People begin saying, "This is how we treat one another," or "This is what matters here." At this point, Creative Altruism is no longer a concept. It is lived. Newcomers feel it. Children absorb it. Visitors carry it elsewhere.

Communities become transmitters of coherence. They translate individual integration into shared practice and shared practice into cultural shift. They are where new ways of living together are tested before they scale.

A world of cooperating communities becomes capable of coordinated evolution.

Quiet Reprise
A community is not built by agreement.
It is built by care,
remembered over time.
When people belong without fear,
differ without division,
and repair without blame,
cooperation becomes home—
and the future finds a place
to grow.

CHAPTER 20

Practices & Patterns of Creative Altruism

Creative Altruism does not live as theory alone. It appears as recognisable patterns—ways of organising creativity, work, and cooperation so that contribution strengthens the whole rather than depleting it. These patterns are not models to copy or standards to enforce. They are shapes that tend to emerge when coherence is allowed to organise itself.

Across different contexts, certain configurations repeat when purpose, care, and intelligence remain in relationship. They are felt before they are formalised. People often recognise them by the ease they bring, the steadiness they support, and the way energy circulates rather than drains.

One such configuration appears in creative projects.

An Altruian creative project does not begin with ownership. It begins with shared purpose. Participants gather around something that cannot be made alone. Roles emerge in response to need rather than status. Contribution is recognised as layered and relational, acknowledged throughout the process rather than negotiated only at the end.

What distinguishes these projects is not the absence of tension, but intelligence in difference. Disagreement is welcomed as information. Decision-making remains close to the work. Care is woven into rhythm rather than appended as afterthought. Under these conditions, creativity sustains itself.

When contribution returns value to those who offer it, energy remains available. Early clarity of purpose, visible attribution, fair participation in outcomes, and repair rather than replacement when tension appears— these are not ideals. They are signals that coherence is present.

A similar pattern appears in organisations.

An Altruian organisation does not optimise people. It supports coherence. Trust is treated as infrastructure, and culture as a living system rather than a set of values to display. Leadership focuses less on control and more on stewardship—protecting clarity, dignity, and rhythm under pressure.

Success in such organisations is not measured by output alone, but by sustainability: retention, learning, resilience, and the capacity to adapt without fragmentation. Structure exists to serve people, not the reverse. Transparent decision pathways, fair recognition of contribution, feedback that refines rather than punishes, and renewal built into rhythm allow people to bring more of themselves—not because they are asked to, but because it feels safe to do so.

Platforms reveal another configuration.

An Altruian platform does not rely on goodwill. It makes goodwill workable. Its design reduces friction for cooperation and increases visibility for contribution. Value flows are legible. Rules are explicit. Participation is rewarded structurally rather than performatively.

Such platforms do not instruct users to behave ethically. They shape an environment in which ethical behaviour becomes the natural outcome of interaction. Attribution is embedded by default. Transparency replaces discretion. Fairness is encoded rather than enforced. Cooperation becomes easier than extraction. Here, culture is taught through design rather than language.

Collectives reveal a further pattern.

An Altruian collective is not a network defined by membership. It is a field shaped by shared orientation. Belonging arises through participation rather than identity. People contribute in different ways and at different times without hierarchy hardening into power. Leadership circulates. Stewardship is shared.

The collective holds memory—of what works, what harms, and what must be protected. Because purpose remains alive, it evolves without losing coherence. Shared purpose revisited regularly, recognition of contribution across roles, conflict held as learning, and continuity valued over growth for its own sake—these allow collectives to become reference points, not because they are visible, but because they feel workable.

Taken together, these patterns do not form a blueprint. They form a sensibility. Wherever Creative Altruism is at work, something similar can be felt: contribution is seen, care is embedded, learning is normal, and renewal is protected. Where these conditions appear, cooperation stabilises without heroics.

Where you see these patterns forming—however imperfectly—Creative Altruism is already alive. Not as doctrine, but as alignment. Not as demand, but as design. The invitation is not to replicate these forms, but to ask what conditions allow them to arise naturally where you are.

Quiet Reprise
Practices endure
when they fit the life
moving through them.
Where contribution is recognised,
where care shapes structure,
and where learning is protected,
coherence settles—
and cooperation
learns how to last.

CHAPTER 21

Playful Cooperation

When Goodwill Learns to Smile

There is often a moment in cooperative work when something shifts. A laugh breaks tension. A playful remark loosens a stuck exchange. An unexpected image opens a conversation that had grown rigid. Nothing of consequence appears to have happened, yet the atmosphere changes. People breathe again. Attention widens. Movement returns.

This is the quiet power of play.

Play is not the opposite of seriousness. It is what allows seriousness to remain human. In cooperative systems, play functions as intelligence—a way of restoring movement, trust, and creativity when effort begins to harden under pressure.

Play alters the field before it alters behaviour. Where play is present, defensiveness softens and curiosity rises. People feel safer to experiment, to offer half-formed ideas, to speak honestly without rehearsing. The nervous system relaxes just enough for intelligence to circulate again.

Without play, cooperation gradually becomes effortful. People monitor themselves more closely. Conversations tighten. Creativity narrows. Even goodwill begins to feel like obligation. When pressure accumulates without release, systems lose elasticity. Play restores it.

Play returns cooperation to the body—to laughter, imagination, spontaneity, and presence. It reminds people that they are not merely roles or functions, but living participants in a shared process. This lightness does not avoid difficulty. It makes difficulty navigable.

Play has always been a form of learning. Children play to understand the world. Animals play to test boundaries and build bonds. Adults play to reconnect with imagination and one another. Play works because it suspends the fear of being wrong. When fear recedes, creativity emerges.

In this sense, play is a gateway to shared intelligence.

Play does not need to be introduced artificially. It often appears naturally when the field is safe. A gentle joke. A sketch instead of an explanation. A question that reframes the moment. These gestures signal that trust is present—that the system can loosen its grip without falling apart.

The role of playful cooperation is not to force fun, but to protect the conditions in which play can arise.

Humour illustrates this well. Not humour that ridicules or deflects, but humour that reveals. The kind that allows truth to be spoken without threat, that acknowledges difficulty without heaviness, that restores perspective without diminishing care. A well-timed laugh can say what careful language cannot. It bypasses ego and speaks directly to shared humanity.

Creativity also depends on risk, and risk depends on safety. Play provides a container where experimentation becomes tolerable. Failure loses its sting. Ideas are offered without over-attachment. Novel connections appear. Play grants permission—to explore, to be unfinished, to not know.

In diverse groups, play often becomes a bridge where words alone fail. Images, stories, gestures, and metaphors create a shared language without demanding uniformity. Difference can express itself without confrontation. Curiosity replaces judgement.

Play does not replace purpose. It serves it. Without purpose, play drifts into distraction. Without play, purpose becomes heavy. Mature cooperation moves fluidly between focus and lightness, seriousness and laughter, effort and ease. This balance keeps systems resilient.

Joy is not the reward for cooperation.
It is the signal that cooperation is working.

When joy appears—quietly or openly—it indicates restored alignment. People feel connected. Energy flows. The field steadies. Joy here is coherence made emotional.

The absence of play is noticeable. Conversations flatten. Creativity thins. Conflict becomes brittle. People remain present physically but withdraw emotionally. When play disappears, it is rarely because people have "grown up." It is because safety has eroded or pressure has exceeded capacity. The response is not forced positivity, but restored trust.

Over time, playful moments become memory. They turn into stories that remind people that cooperation can be joyful, that difficulty can be met lightly, and that shared humanity matters. These memories become cultural glue, carrying tone long after the moment has passed.

At its deepest level, play is an expression of care. It says: you are safe here. We can explore together. You do not have to perform to belong. In this way, play becomes a form of social compassion—keeping cooperation humane as systems grow more complex.

Quiet Reprise
Play opens
what pressure closes.
It reminds intelligence
how to move.
When goodwill learns to smile,
cooperation lightens,
creativity grows braver,
and the field remembers
that joy is not extra—
it is essential.

CHAPTER 22

Breakdowns and Breakthroughs

When What Falls Apart Is Making Space

Every living system reaches moments when what once worked no longer does. A conversation stalls. A team loses energy. A person feels depleted, confused, or misaligned. These moments are often labelled as breakdowns and treated as problems to fix, disruptions to manage, or failures to overcome.

Creative Altruism approaches them differently.

A breakdown is not a sign that something has gone wrong. It is a sign that something has outgrown the structure holding it. What is breaking down is not life itself, but an arrangement that no longer fits the energy moving through it.

Breakdowns occur when existing forms—habits, roles, processes, identities—can no longer carry what is being asked of them. For a time, these forms provided stability. Then life continued. Complexity increased. Relationship deepened. Eventually, the structure became too small.

When this happens, friction appears. People feel tired rather than inspired. Communication grows strained. Meaning thins. Creativity withdraws. Effort increases while results decline. These are not moral failures. They are signals of misalignment.

A breakdown is life saying, quietly but firmly: *this no longer fits here.*

The most important moment in any breakdown is rarely the crisis itself. It is the instant before reaction. When discomfort arises, the impulse is to push harder, assign blame, fix quickly, or retreat into control. These responses are understandable. They are survival reflexes. But they often deepen the fracture.

Breakdowns require something counterintuitive: pause.

Pausing interrupts the reflex to defend. It creates space for perception. It allows the system to feel what is actually happening rather than immediately imposing a solution. In this space, intelligence has a chance to return.

Every breakdown carries information. It may be revealing that purpose has faded into routine, that care has been sacrificed for speed, that intelligence has become clever but disconnected, or that trust has been stretched without renewal. The breakdown does not tell us how to fix things. It tells us where relationship has been lost.

When met with curiosity rather than panic, breakdowns become teachers.

Because breakdowns touch meaning, they often stir emotion. Disappointment, anger, shame, fear, or exhaustion surface not because people are weak, but because something they care about feels threatened. Emotion here is not noise. It is data.

In integrative systems, emotion is allowed to surface without being weaponised. People are invited to name what they feel—not to dramatise it, but to make it visible. A single honest sentence can change the field:

Something feels off. I'm overwhelmed. I don't feel heard. I'm afraid we're losing what mattered. Such statements return humanity to the centre of the moment.

In groups, breakdowns often express themselves as conflict. Conflict is rarely about the surface issue. It points to unmet needs, unspoken fears, or misaligned values. Avoided, conflict festers. Confronted aggressively, it polarises. Held with goodwill, it becomes *creative tension.*

Creative Altruism does not aim to eliminate conflict. It seeks to integrate it—allowing difference to inform redesign rather than fragment relationship. Breakthroughs emerge not when conflict disappears, but when people feel safe enough to stay present within it.

There is often a threshold moment in every breakdown where two paths diverge. One leads to contraction—blame, withdrawal, rigidity, repetition. The other opens toward expansion—insight, redesign, honesty, renewal. The difference between these paths is not skill or intelligence. It is willingness to learn.

When a system chooses learning over defence, energy locked in tension becomes available for creativity. What felt like collapse begins to feel like reorganisation.

Breakthroughs are often quieter than expected. They arrive not with certainty, but with relief. Conversation simplifies. A sense of direction returns. Nothing external may have changed yet, but the field has. Purpose, care, and intelligence have re-entered relationship.

Many breakdowns occur not because systems are flawed, but because renewal has been neglected. Cooperation requires rest, reflection, and recalibration. Without these, even aligned systems exhaust themselves.

Renewal does not demand retreat. It asks for honesty—a pause, a conversation, a rearticulation of purpose, a simplification of process, a moment of gratitude.

Renewal restores elasticity. Without it, systems snap.

Leadership is revealed in breakdowns. Not through answers or authority, but through presence. An integrative leader slows the system down, names what is happening, protects dignity, invites truth, and holds space until coherence begins to return. Over time, in mature systems, this capacity spreads. Groups learn to hold themselves through difficulty without fragmentation.

When breakdowns are met with care and intelligence, systems do not return to how they were. They evolve. Trust deepens. Communication cleans. Structure simplifies. Purpose clarifies. Resilience increases. What once felt like failure becomes foundation.

This is why Creative Altruism does not fear breakdowns. It respects them as evolutionary moments.

At a wider scale, many of the challenges of our time are collective breakdowns—signals that old systems can no longer carry the complexity of our interconnected world. These, too, are thresholds. The same principles apply: pause, listen, integrate, redesign. The same forces are present: purpose, care, and intelligence.

Breakdowns prepare the ground for wisdom.

Quiet Reprise
Breakdowns are not endings.
They are openings.
When what no longer fits
is allowed to fall away,
space appears—
and life finds a new way
to move through us.

CHAPTER 23

Wayfinding

Learning to Move Without a Map

There are times when the old maps stop working. Paths that once felt reliable begin to blur. Decisions that used to come easily now carry weight. The future no longer unfolds along predictable lines. This is often experienced as confusion or loss of direction. Yet it is more accurately a sign of transition.

Wayfinding begins when certainty dissolves and attention deepens.

Maps assume stability. They function best when terrain is known and change is gradual. In living systems—especially those shaped by accelerating cultural, technological, and relational shifts—maps age quickly. The moment they are drawn, the landscape has already changed.

Wayfinding does not reject planning. It places planning in its proper relationship to life.

Rather than asking *Where exactly are we going?* wayfinding asks *What direction feels aligned now?* Rather than demanding certainty, it cultivates orientation. Orientation is not a destination. It is a felt sense of coherence—a recognition that the next step belongs, even if the whole path is not yet visible.

Every person carries an inner compass. It is not mystical. It is composed of familiar capacities: awareness, empathy, discernment, and intention. When these are in conversation, direction emerges naturally. Wayfinding begins when people slow just enough to sense this alignment.

Does this step feel expansive or contracting?
Does it clarify or confuse?
Does it strengthen relationship or strain it?
Does it increase coherence in the field?

These questions are experiential. The body, emotions, and intuition often register orientation before the mind can articulate it. Wayfinding trusts this sensitivity—not as impulse, but as information.

One of the challenges of wayfinding is learning to act without full visibility. Modern culture trains people to wait for certainty, yet living systems rarely offer it. Clarity often appears after movement, not before. Wayfinding invites trust in partial visibility—the courage to take a step without demanding the entire route.

This is not recklessness. It is responsiveness.

When purpose is present and care intact, small steps are sufficient. Each step reveals something. Adjustment follows. Movement and learning remain in dialogue.

Wayfinding is rarely solitary. In teams and communities, navigation becomes relational. Direction is sensed together, not through debate over opinions, but through attention to the field. Energy, tension, curiosity, and resistance all carry information. When groups pause to notice what is emerging rather than forcing agreement, a shared orientation often appears. It may be provisional. It may change. But it feels alive.

There are moments when even orientation fades. Fatigue sets in. Discouragement surfaces. People are unsure what matters anymore. In such moments, the impulse is often to push harder or withdraw entirely. Both deepen disconnection.

Wayfinding offers a gentler response: return to first questions.

Why are we here?
What do we care about?
What do we want to protect?

Direction often reappears not through new goals, but through remembered values.

Wayfinding also involves a particular quality of listening—not only to what is present, but to what is trying to emerge. Signals are subtle: a recurring question, a persistent discomfort, an unexpected invitation, a shift in tone, a conversation that lingers. These are not instructions. They are invitations. Learning to listen forward allows people to sense possibility before it fully takes form.

In this mode, decisions become experiments rather than declarations. A step is taken. The system responds. Information returns. Adjustment follows. This posture reduces fear. Mistakes become data. Curiosity replaces self-protection. Humility becomes practical.

In uncertain terrain, wayfinding relies on a steady reference point. In Creative Altruism, that reference is goodwill. When options feel complex, the question *Which choice strengthens relationship and coherence?* often cuts through confusion. Goodwill does not provide answers to every problem. It orients intention.

Timing matters as much as direction. Some moments ask for action. Others ask for patience, rest, or restraint. Wayfinding requires sensitivity to rhythm—the capacity to sense when to move and when to wait. Forcing action too early exhausts systems. Delaying action too long dulls momentum. Rhythm keeps navigation humane.

Leadership in wayfinding contexts changes shape. The leader is not the one who knows the route. It is the one who holds orientation when others feel uncertain—who protects values, steadies the field, and allows clarity to emerge. This leadership listens deeply, acts lightly, and adjusts often.

At a wider scale, humanity itself is engaged in collective wayfinding. Old certainties are dissolving. New systems are forming. Ecological, technological, and cultural challenges require navigation without precedent. The same principles apply: pause rather than panic, listen rather than impose, learn rather than defend, cooperate rather than compete.

You can often tell when wayfinding is working. Movement feels purposeful rather than frantic. Decisions feel timely rather than forced. Learning replaces blame. Trust deepens. The field steadies. The path may remain uncertain, but it feels viable.

Quiet Reprise
When the map dissolves,
attention sharpens.
Guided by care,
aligned by purpose,
and refined through listening,
we discover that the path
does not need to be known—
only felt—
one honest step
at a time.

CHAPTER 24

Stories and Transmission

How What We Live Begins to Travel

Nothing meaningful spreads because it is explained well. It spreads because it is recognised. Long before ideas are adopted, they are felt. Long before principles are articulated, they are embodied. Creative Altruism does not move through persuasion or instruction. It moves through transmission—the quiet process by which coherence in one place awakens coherence in another.

Transmission begins before language.

Transmission is guided not only by what is said, but by what is desirable. People are drawn toward ways of being that feel workable, human, and alive. Long before a story persuades, it attracts. Long before principles are adopted, tone is recognised. What spreads most reliably is not conviction, but coherence—felt as ease, steadiness, and the quiet sense that it is good to be here.

It is carried in tone, timing, and presence. In the way someone listens without interrupting. In how disagreement is handled without escalation. In the steadiness shown when pressure mounts. People often say they were influenced by someone, but what they mean is that something shifted in that person's presence. A sense of ease. A clarity. A grounded kindness that felt real rather than performed.

This is transmission at its most basic: coherence becoming visible.

Stories matter because they allow recognition to travel. Human beings understand themselves through story, not as instruction, but as resonance. A story does not tell us what to think. It invites us to remember what we already know. When we hear of cooperation that worked, of care reshaping a difficult situation, of integrity held quietly under strain, something inside us leans forward.

Possibility becomes imaginable.

The stories that transmit most effectively are rarely dramatic. They are small, human moments: a leader admitting a mistake; a team pausing instead of pushing; a conflict resolved through listening rather than dominance; a community choosing care over convenience. These stories do not create heroes. They reveal ways of being together that feel workable.

Their power lies in their ordinariness.

Transmission happens most reliably through example. People learn less from what is declared than from what is practised consistently. When someone responds to tension with curiosity instead of defence, the field shifts. When someone shares credit without calculation, it recalibrates what feels normal. When someone chooses honesty even when it costs them, others notice.

Transmission travels through the field. The relational atmosphere that forms wherever people gather carries information long before words do. A coherent field invites openness. A brittle field closes it. People do not absorb new ways of working in environments that feel unsafe. They absorb them where dignity is protected and care is present.

This is why kindness is not peripheral in Creative Altruism. It is a medium of transmission.

There is a form of teaching that does not announce itself. It appears when someone asks a better question, slows a conversation at the right moment, or reframes conflict without blame. Nothing is labelled. Nothing is formal. Yet learning occurs. People take what feels usable and leave the rest.

Creative Altruism travels this way—not through authority, but through invitation.

Transmission also moves through generations. Children learn cooperation by experiencing it. Young people learn integrity by witnessing it. Elders pass on wisdom not through explanation, but through presence and story. When Creative Altruism becomes part of daily life, expectations shift quietly. What feels normal changes. Culture begins to turn.

Technology plays a role here, not as driver, but as carrier. Stories now travel farther and faster than ever before. Technology amplifies what is already present. When guided by fear, it spreads fear. When guided by ego, it spreads outrage. When guided by care, it can carry coherence. The medium matters less than the tone it transmits.

Transmission distorts when language detaches from practice. Words hollow when repeated without embodiment. Creative Altruism guards against this not through control, but through humility. Transmission remains alive when people continue listening, learning, and adapting— when no one claims ownership of the truth.

What is lived stays honest.

What is only spoken drifts.

Becoming a carrier of Creative Altruism does not require a platform. It happens whenever someone chooses coherence over reaction, care over convenience, and honesty over performance. It is expressed in how one enters a room, how one leaves it, and what remains in the field afterward.

Over time, these moments accumulate. Patterns form. Patterns shape culture. Culture influences systems. This is how Creative Altruism spreads—not by replication, but by resonance.

People do not copy behaviour.
They adopt orientation.

As transmission deepens, something shifts. Cooperation feels practical. Trust becomes normal. Alignment replaces enforcement. A different future becomes conceivable, not because it was argued into place, but because it was lived into being.

Quiet Reprise
What we live
travels farther
than what we say.
Through presence,
through story,
through the way we meet one another,
coherence learns to move—
and the future
quietly begins to listen.

CHAPTER 25

Transmission in Action

When Coherence Begins to Shape the World

There comes a moment when something quiet becomes noticeable. A way of listening begins to influence decisions. A tone of care alters how power is exercised. A habit of reflection reshapes how work unfolds. Nothing dramatic announces this shift, yet Creative Altruism is no longer only personal or relational. It has begun to act.

Transmission in action does not look like activism or enforcement. It does not arrive with slogans or campaigns. It carries a different quality— one that can be felt more easily than described. Action begins to feel guided rather than driven. Integrity no longer requires effort to maintain. Things move with less force.

People notice this first in how work feels. Meetings resolve more cleanly. Conflict dissipates sooner. Creativity returns where it had stalled. Outcomes still matter. Responsibility remains. But the path forward feels steadier, as though the system itself has begun to cooperate. This is how coherence expresses itself externally.

Often, the earliest signs appear through behaviour that others begin to mirror. Someone pauses before responding, and the room follows. Someone speaks plainly without blame, and the tone shifts. Someone admits uncertainty, and permission spreads. These moments are small, but they re-pattern the field. Without instruction, people adjust to what now feels possible.

Transmission in action works through contagious normality.

In organisations, transmission in action often registers as a change in atmosphere before any formal shift occurs. People speak more freely. Information flows more openly. Credit is shared more generously. Feedback arrives earlier and lands more cleanly. Over time, these behavioural changes begin shaping outcomes—retention improves, creativity increases, and trust becomes a tangible asset. Yet what people often notice first is relief.

Decisions made within this orientation carry a different weight. They consider impact beyond immediate advantage. They ask how outcomes will affect relationship, dignity, and long-term coherence. This does not slow progress. It often accelerates it by reducing rework, resistance, and regret. Good decisions feel light because they do not leave emotional debris behind. Leadership, under these conditions, feels less like command and more like stewardship.

At the level of community, transmission in action rarely begins with formal initiatives. It begins with people stepping forward naturally. Someone organises a gathering. Someone bridges a disagreement. Others join not because they were persuaded, but because the invitation feels right. Mobilisation happens without polarisation.

As Creative Altruism moves into visible form, a subtle ethical responsibility appears. Visibility can invite distortion. What is meant to be lived can become displayed. What is meant to serve can become claimed. Transmission in action remains healthy when humility stays present—when listening continues, learning remains active, and adaptation replaces certainty.

Over time, isolated actions become patterns. Patterns stabilise into culture. Culture shapes systems. Systems influence lives. This is how Creative Altruism scales—not through replication, but through resonance. People do not adopt actions wholesale. They adopt orientation.

Perhaps the clearest sign that transmission has moved into action is how it feels. People feel less alone. Work feels meaningful without being heavy. Conflict feels workable. Hope becomes realistic. These are not abstractions. They are lived indicators that coherence is beginning to shape the world.

Quiet Reprise
When coherence acts,
the world responds.
Through simple choices,
through steady presence,
through action that does not betray its source,
what was once personal
becomes practical—
and the future
finds its footing
in how we choose to move
today.

PART IV

Toward the Altruian Age

Extending Creative Altruism into culture, systems, economy and the future.

CHAPTER 26

The Altruian Field

When Many Become More Than the Sum of Their Parts

There are moments when something intangible becomes unmistakably real. A group settles into shared focus. Insight appears between people rather than coming from any one of them. No one is directing this. No one is performing it. Yet something coherent is clearly present.

This is what is meant by the Altruian Field.

Most people encounter the field long before they have language for it. They describe it indirectly—*It felt different in that room. We were really aligned. Everything just flowed.* These phrases point to a shared recognition: whenever people gather, an atmosphere forms. This atmosphere shapes how they think, speak, decide, and relate, often more powerfully than plans or policies.

The Altruian Field is simply a coherent atmosphere—one shaped by purpose, care, and intelligent relationship.

The field does not arise because people agree. It forms when people are present. Presence allows listening. Listening allows trust. Trust allows difference. Difference allows intelligence. When these conditions align, something collective becomes accessible. The field becomes a container capable of holding many perspectives without fragmentation.

Human beings regulate one another continuously, often without awareness. Tone spreads. Calm steadies. Anxiety amplifies. In groups, this creates a shared nervous system. When the system is overstimulated, reaction dominates. When it is regulated, response becomes possible. The Altruian Field supports this regulation. It slows what needs slowing and energises what needs movement.

This is why coherence feels calming without becoming passive, and energising without becoming frantic.

One of the most striking qualities of a coherent field is how intelligence changes shape. Ideas stop competing. Insights begin to build. Decisions arrive with less debate. People often say, *We were thinking together.* They were. When defensiveness relaxes and attention is shared, intelligence becomes collective rather than private.

The field allows intelligence to move between people.

The field is sensitive. It weakens when communication grows unclear, when power is exercised without care, when urgency replaces meaning, or when listening diminishes. None of this happens suddenly. Fields fray gradually. The first sign is often a subtle heaviness—conversations feel harder, creativity stalls, people withdraw emotionally.

One of the most important practices within Creative Altruism is field repair. Repair does not require analysis or strategy. It requires honesty. Naming tension. Offering apology without defence. Restating purpose. Pausing long enough to breathe together. Such gestures often restore coherence with surprising speed.

Healthy systems repair early and often.

Every coherent field has stewards—people who sense atmosphere and respond accordingly. They are not always leaders by role. Often they are the ones who notice when energy drops, slow conversations at the right moment, ask clarifying questions, bring warmth without control, or protect dignity under pressure. Stewardship is not authority. It is attentiveness combined with care.

In mature fields, stewardship spreads. Everyone contributes to coherence.

The Altruian Field is not limited by proximity. It can form across distance, including digital space, when intention is clear and care is present. Technology becomes a carrier rather than a barrier. What matters is not closeness of bodies, but quality of relationship. The field follows attention.

When the field remains coherent over time, something deeper emerges: belonging. People feel seen without performance. Difference is welcomed without fear. Contribution feels meaningful. The field becomes an emotional home—a place where people can be themselves while participating in something larger.

As more people experience and cultivate coherent fields, these fields begin to connect. Practices spread. Norms shift. Creative Altruism scales through resonance. People recognise what feels alive and seek it out. Organisations adopt what works. Communities learn from one another. The field teaches without instruction.

As humanity becomes more interconnected, the ability to cultivate coherent fields will shape the future more profoundly than any single technology or policy. Leadership depends on it. Education relies on it. Culture is carried by it. The Altruian Field is not an abstraction.

It is the medium through which cooperation becomes possible at scale.

Quiet Reprise
The field we create
creates us in return.
Held by purpose,
nourished by care,
and shaped through attention,
it becomes a quiet intelligence—
guiding many voices
into a shared song
of becoming.

CHAPTER 27

The Spiritual and Inner Framework

The Quiet Alignment That Holds Everything Together

Behind every cooperative act—every moment of clarity, kindness, or shared intelligence—there is an inner condition. Not a belief to adopt or a doctrine to defend, but an alignment quietly shaping how a person meets life. When this alignment is present, behaviour changes without effort. Listening deepens. Reaction softens. Timing becomes more sensitive.

This chapter turns inward to that condition—not as spirituality in the conventional sense, but as lived coherence: the inner ground that allows Creative Altruism to express itself through a human life.

Many hesitate around the word *spiritual* because it has been burdened with belief systems, hierarchies, and histories that no longer fit the conditions we inhabit. Here, spirituality is simpler and more exacting. It refers to the quality of relationship between thought, feeling, intention, and action. It is the degree to which a person is present enough to act with clarity and care, even under pressure.

Spirituality, in this sense, is not added to life.
It is what remains when fragmentation falls away.

Every person carries an inner architecture. Thought interprets. Feeling senses. Intention directs. When these operate in isolation, life feels disjointed. People overthink without acting, feel without clarity, or act without reflection. Stress increases. Meaning thins. When these dimensions begin to cooperate, something steadies. Decisions simplify. Emotion becomes informative rather than overwhelming. Action aligns more naturally with values.

This cooperation is inner integration—the spiritual foundation of Creative Altruism.

Presence is the doorway to this integration. Presence does not require special states or long retreats. It appears whenever attention returns to what is actually happening—in the body, in the conversation, in the moment. A breath noticed. A pause before responding. A moment of listening without preparing an answer. These small acts restore contact with reality.

Presence interrupts reactivity.
It allows intelligence to catch up with emotion.
It softens the impulse to control.

Just as groups generate a field between people, individuals carry an inner field—an atmosphere shaped by habits of attention, self-talk, emotional patterns, and values. Some inner fields feel rushed or tense. Others feel calm but withdrawn. Some feel scattered. Others feel grounded and open. The quality of this inner field matters. It shapes how we enter relationship, how we handle conflict, and how we contribute to collective environments.

Inner coherence strengthens outer fields.

Inner listening develops this coherence. It is a gentle skill—the capacity to notice signals without immediately acting on them. Fatigue, resistance, curiosity, excitement, fear: each carries information. Instead of asking how to eliminate these signals, inner listening asks what they are revealing. Emotion shifts from disturbance to guidance. Thought shifts from dominance to clarity. Intention becomes responsive rather than rigid.

Wisdom emerges this way.

Intention itself is often misunderstood as willpower. In Creative Altruism, intention is orientation—the quiet commitment to act in ways that strengthen coherence rather than fracture it. A simple inner question often reveals intention clearly: *What matters most here?* When intention is present, action simplifies. When it is absent, effort multiplies.

As alignment deepens, resistance inevitably appears. Old habits surface. Fear questions change. Doubt tests resolve. This is not failure. It is integration in motion. Resistance once served a protective function. Energy once tied up in self-protection becomes available for creativity.

Honesty plays a subtle but central role here. Not harsh self-judgement, but the willingness to name what is true internally—what is felt, what is wanted, what is feared, what is avoided. When inner truth is acknowledged, tension releases. When it is suppressed, fragmentation grows. A person who can tell the truth inwardly can speak it kindly outwardly.

Stillness supports this process. Without moments of stillness, attention fragments. Without rest, presence thins. Without reflection, learning stalls. Stillness does not mean withdrawal. It means allowing space for experience to settle and meaning to surface. A walk without agenda. A few quiet minutes. A day without performance. These are not indulgences. They are structural.

Stillness recalibrates alignment.

Service, when grounded in this inner coherence, changes character. It is no longer sacrifice, but expression. Contribution flows from alignment rather than obligation. People give without depletion, care without resentment, and remain human under pressure. This is spiritual maturity in practice—action arising from coherence rather than demand.

Inner alignment is not private. It radiates. A person who is present regulates rooms. A person who is grounded steadies conflict. A person who is clear simplifies complexity. Inner coherence shapes the field others enter, influencing culture without instruction.

As systems grow more complex, this inner foundation becomes more important, not less. Complexity amplifies fragmentation where it exists and reveals maturity where it has been cultivated. The spiritual and inner framework of Creative Altruism allows individuals to remain humane inside complexity.

With this inner coherence in view, the movement ahead turns toward continuity—how integration is carried through time without hardening, and how what is lived remains alive beyond the moment.

Quiet Reprise
When thought listens,
when feeling informs,
and when intention steadies action,
the inner world aligns—
and life moves forward
with less force
and more grace.

CHAPTER 28

Integration and Continuity

How Coherence Is Carried Through Time

Much of what has been explored so far concerns integration: the quiet intelligence by which creativity, care, and cooperation learn to move together without force. Integration explains how coherence appears— within individuals, between people, and across systems. Yet something further is required if coherence is to matter beyond moments of insight.

That requirement is continuity.

Integration gives coherence its form.
Continuity gives coherence its life.

Many experiences feel true when first encountered. Moments of clarity arise. Conversations align. Work feels meaningful again. But insight alone does not endure. Without continuity, even the most compelling orientation fades under pressure, fatigue, disagreement, or time.

Continuity is the difference between an experience that inspires and a way of being that sustains.

In Creative Altruism, continuity is not about maintaining a fixed state. It is about *holding relationship over time*—between purpose and action, between care and decision-making, between intelligence and humility. Where integration brings elements into conversation, continuity keeps that conversation alive as conditions change.

This distinction matters because many systems do not fail through bad intention. They fragment through drift. Purpose becomes implicit rather than remembered. Care is assumed rather than practised. Intelligence turns procedural rather than responsive.

Small misalignments accumulate quietly until coherence thins into effort, cynicism, or exhaustion. By the time breakdown is visible, relationship has often been lost for some time. Continuity is what notices this early.

Living systems sustain themselves through rhythm rather than control. They move through cycles of alignment, expression, strain, reflection, and renewal. When this rhythm is honoured, systems mature. When it is ignored, they harden or collapse. Continuity does not resist change; it carries coherence *through* change. Continuity is not conservative. It is adaptive.

Within individuals, continuity appears as the ability to return to presence after reactivity, to purpose after distraction. An integrated person is not one who never fragments, but one who notices fragmentation quickly and knows how to come back. Over time, this return becomes instinctive. Integrity stabilises not because perfection is achieved, but because repair is normal.

Between people, continuity appears as trust. Trust does not mean agreement or comfort. It means confidence that difference can be held without rupture, that tension will be met with care, and that truth will not be punished. Groups with continuity do not avoid difficulty; they metabolise it. Disagreement becomes navigational rather than adversarial. Conflict becomes information rather than threat.

At the level of teams and organisations, continuity becomes cultural memory. It lives in how breakdowns are handled, how learning is retained, how decisions are revisited, and how renewal is protected. A system with continuity remembers what matters even as roles change, people leave, and circumstances shift. Without this memory, values become slogans and principles lose traction.

Continuity requires anchors—but not rules.

Anchors are simple, repeatable acts that return attention to what matters:

- a purpose spoken aloud,
- a pause taken before escalation,
- a conversation reopened rather than avoided,
- a rhythm of reflection that is respected rather than postponed.

These anchors do not constrain creativity. They protect it.

Change, when held by continuity, becomes refinement. New structures can appear without erasing relational intelligence. Scale can increase without soul thinning. Technology can be introduced without overriding judgement. Continuity allows systems to evolve without forgetting themselves.

This capacity becomes increasingly critical as complexity intensifies. Ecological strain, technological acceleration, cultural fragmentation, and economic pressure all test whether coherence can be sustained under load. Integration alone is not enough. Without continuity, coherence remains fragile—dependent on individuals rather than embedded in shared practice.

Continuity is what allows Creative Altruism to move from insight into inheritance.

When continuity is present, coherence becomes recognisable through tone, timing, and behaviour. Newcomers feel it. Children absorb it. Systems carry it forward even when no one is explicitly teaching it. What endures becomes transmissible.

In this sense, continuity is leadership—not as authority, but as stewardship. It is the willingness to protect the conditions under which care, creativity, and cooperation can remain in relationship over time. It is the courage to slow when speed would fracture, and to remember purpose when habit takes over.

Quiet Reprise
Integration gives coherence form.
Continuity gives coherence time.
When we return—again and again—
to purpose without rigidity, to care without sentiment,
and to intelligence without arrogance,
what works does not disappear.
It deepens.

CHAPTER 29

Futures of Altruia

The Emerging Civilisation Already Taking Shape

The future rarely arrives as an event. It arrives as a change in tone. Long before structures shift, people begin listening differently. Long before systems transform, assumptions soften. What follows is not prediction, but recognition—an attempt to notice what is already taking form beneath the surface of daily life.

Many sense this shift not as excitement, but as relief. Not as certainty, but as a quiet recognition that familiar ways of organising work, value, and success no longer feel convincing. They still function, but they no longer hold trust. Alongside this erosion, new patterns appear—tentative, imperfect, and alive.

People begin choosing collaboration where rivalry once felt automatic. They question extraction without needing to be persuaded. They orient toward coherence rather than dominance. These movements do not yet constitute a new civilisation. They constitute its conditions.

As Creative Altruism moves from idea to lived practice, something else begins to happen quietly. New forms of work and contribution start to emerge — roles that do not fit neatly into existing job descriptions, yet are essential to a cooperative economy. People find themselves acting as bridges, facilitators, interpreters, and stewards of shared purpose. These are not professions designed in advance, but vocations that arise naturally when creativity, care, and cooperation are placed at the centre of value creation. In time, such roles may become more visible and more widely recognised. For now, they remain one of the understated signals that a different way of working — and a different way of being — is already taking shape.

THE CONVERGENCE OF A GLOBAL IMPULSE

As the conditions of the Altruian Age begin to take shape, interest in the principles and practices of Creative Altruism naturally accelerates. Across cultures, disciplines, and domains of work, people are arriving — often independently — at similar recognitions: that creativity cannot thrive without care, that cooperation outperforms rivalry in complex systems, and that altruism must become structural rather than exceptional.

This convergence is not coincidence.
It is response.

When an orientation reflects a genuine need of its time, it tends to surface in many places at once. The emergence of Creative Altruism is best understood not as the success of a single framework, but as the awakening of a shared intelligence — one learning how to organise human effort differently under new conditions.

With this emergence comes responsibility.

If Creative Altruism is to fulfil its promise, it must remain faithful to its own principles. Care must extend not only outward, but inward — into how initiatives relate to one another. Cooperation must guide not only projects, but the architecture of the field itself. Creativity must be expressed not as competition for ownership, but as shared exploration.

One of the risks at this stage is not disagreement, but fragmentation —
the quiet erosion of coherence through rivalry, duplication, and fear.

The invitation of the Altruian Age is different.

It asks those working in the spirit of Creative Altruism to recognise one
another as allies; to share language rather than guard it; and to join hands
in shaping a global framework that is diverse in expression yet unified in
orientation. Not a single organisation, but a living symphony — many
voices, many approaches, held together by shared care for the whole.

Creative Altruism is not something to be claimed.
It is something to be stewarded.
And stewardship, in this age, begins with cooperation.

One of the clearest signs of this transition is a subtle reorientation
from extraction toward contribution. For generations, progress was
measured by what could be taken—resources, labour, attention,
advantage. This logic delivered growth, but it carried costs that are
now felt in bodies, relationships, and environments. Burnout replaces
motivation. Abundance coexists with anxiety. Efficiency increases while
meaning thins.

In response, a different question begins to matter: *does this strengthen the
whole?* Contribution is not self-sacrifice. It is participation in a system
that can sustain itself. When people begin asking whether value returns
to those who create it, whether work increases life or drains it, a
civilisational pivot quietly begins.

As complexity increases, competition loses effectiveness as a primary organiser. Challenges no longer sit neatly within silos. Ecological, technological, cultural, and economic realities interweave. Under these conditions, cooperation re-emerges—not as moral appeal, but as necessity. In teams it appears as faster learning. In organisations, as lower friction. In communities, as resilience. Cooperation reveals itself as intelligence.

Technology, too, begins to behave differently when guided by this orientation. It has always amplified the consciousness behind it. Where extraction dominates, it accelerates inequality. Where care and clarity are present, it extends possibility. Across many fields, technology is quietly being reimagined—not as a tool for control, but as a partner in cooperation. Platforms begin rewarding contribution rather than outrage. Systems privilege transparency over opacity. Design attends to wellbeing alongside efficiency. This does not require perfect ethics. It requires direction.

Work is often the first domain where these shifts become visible. The old tension between survival and meaning grows intolerable. People no longer accept that contribution must come at the cost of dignity, or that success requires exhaustion. New rhythms appear—shared ownership, cooperative teams, flexible structures, transparent decision-making, and an understanding of wellbeing as capacity rather than indulgence.

Ambition does not disappear.
It refines.

As contribution replaces extraction, economic life begins to feel more ecological. Value circulates rather than accumulates. Resources regenerate rather than deplete. Economies are understood less as machines to optimise and more as living systems to tend. Fairness becomes practical.

These changes do not arise from theory.
They arise from lived necessity.

Communities play a central role in this emergence. Large-scale transformation rarely begins at scale. It begins in neighbourhoods, collectives, and shared projects where new ways of living together are tested before they spread. Communities become civilisational cells— places where cooperation is learned, refined, and transmitted.

Leadership shifts accordingly. Authority moves away from domination and toward coherence. People trust those who listen, follow those who steady the field, and respect those who protect dignity under pressure. Leadership becomes stewardship: the capacity to hold purpose, care, and intelligence in relationship.

Education, too, begins to reorient. Less toward accumulation of information, more toward cultivation of capacity. Young people learn how to regulate emotion, collaborate across difference, think systemically, act ethically under uncertainty, and care for shared resources. Learning becomes preparation for relationship, not merely employment.

As these patterns stabilise, measures of progress change. Output and speed no longer stand alone. Wellbeing, trust, coherence, creativity, resilience, and dignity become meaningful indicators of systemic health. These are not sentimental values. They are signals of maturity.

The Altruian Age does not arrive by declaration. It emerges through practice—through people choosing cooperation where competition no longer serves, designing systems for fairness rather than extraction, aligning technology with life, and remembering joy as a civilisational resource. No single institution controls this emergence. No ideology defines it.

Perhaps the most significant shift is this: people stop waiting for the future to arrive. They recognise that they are already standing inside it— shaping it through daily choices, relationships, and designs. The future is not ahead of us. It is forming through us.

Quiet Reprise
The future does not announce itself.
It recognises itself.
In every act of cooperation,
in every system shaped with care,
in every choice that strengthens the whole,
a new civilisation takes its first breath—
again and again—
through the lives of those
already living it.

CHAPTER 30

Scaling Without Losing Soul

How What Matters Stays Human as It Grows

Growth changes things. What once felt intimate becomes complex. What once moved through trust alone begins to require structure. Many systems falter here—not because their intentions were wrong, but because expansion outruns care.

In early stages, cooperation feels effortless. People know one another. Decisions are close to the work. Culture lives in tone rather than policy. The soul of the system is carried through proximity and shared experience. As growth occurs, these conditions shift. New people arrive who were not present at the beginning. Decisions are made at distance. Processes appear to replace conversation. Metrics begin to stand in for meaning. Nothing has failed. Yet something precious feels at risk.

When growth reaches this point, it becomes a test—not of ambition, but of integrity.

Soul, as it is used here, is not sentiment. It is the felt humanity of a system—the qualities that allow people to feel seen rather than processed, trusted rather than managed. A system with soul feels purposeful rather than performative, relational rather than transactional. When soul thins, people may still perform, but they no longer belong.

Soul is rarely lost through malice alone. It erodes through neglect.

Speed overtakes listening. Efficiency replaces reflection. Structure grows faster than relationship. Under these conditions, systems default to control. Control produces compliance. Compliance creates distance. Distance drains trust. What disappears is not capability, but connection.

Scaling without losing soul does not mean resisting growth. It means allowing growth to be guided by the same qualities that made the work worth growing. In living systems, expansion is always paired with integration. Roots deepen as branches spread. Circulation adjusts as size increases. Human systems require the same intelligence.

As scale increases, purpose can no longer remain implicit. What was once understood must be remembered aloud. People who arrive later cannot intuit original intention. They must encounter it—not as branding, but as lived orientation. When purpose is re-spoken regularly, growth feels anchored. When it is assumed, drift begins.

Culture cannot be delegated. It is not preserved by documents or slogans. It is transmitted through behaviour, especially under pressure. How leaders respond to tension. How mistakes are handled. How credit is shared. How newcomers are welcomed. These moments teach more than any handbook. When culture is treated as someone else's responsibility, it disappears.

Structure becomes unavoidable as systems grow. The question is not whether to introduce structure, but what that structure serves. Structure designed solely for efficiency eventually exhausts people. Structure designed to protect clarity, fairness, rhythm, and dignity frees energy. At its best, structure becomes an act of care.

Leadership plays a crucial role here. Scaling with soul requires leaders who regulate pace rather than chase speed, who sense when renewal is needed, and who protect relational warmth under pressure. Such leadership may appear cautious. In reality, it is guardianship—holding long-term coherence through short-term strain.

Metrics inevitably enter at scale. They can inform decisions, but they can also distort them. When metrics replace conversation, soul thins. When numbers speak louder than lived experience, people feel invisible. Some of the most important indicators are felt before they are measured: fatigue, cynicism, silence, loss of joy. Listening to these signals is an act of intelligence.

Scaling with soul also requires discernment about limits. Not everything should grow. Some practices lose power when expanded indiscriminately. Some relationships require intimacy. Some decisions must remain local. The courage to keep certain things human-sized is not failure. It is maturity.

When growth is held well, something remarkable happens. People feel proud to belong. Culture deepens instead of diluting. Expansion becomes expression rather than accumulation.

At a broader level, this question echoes across civilisation. Can humanity scale technology, economies, and institutions without losing its humanity? The answer will not come from optimisation alone. It will come from coherence.

Creative Altruism offers a direction—not a guarantee—toward growth that remains relational, ethical, and alive.

Quiet Reprise

Growth reveals what we value.

Scale amplifies what we practise.

When purpose is remembered,

when care shapes structure,

and when intelligence listens before it accelerates,

what grows does not lose its soul—

it gains room

to breathe.

CHAPTER 31

Technology and the Soul of Scale

When Intelligence Is Asked to Remember What It Serves

After growth comes amplification. What begins as a human way of working—a tone of care, a habit of listening, a culture of cooperation— eventually encounters technology. Tools appear to manage complexity. Systems are introduced to handle volume and distance. Automation promises relief from strain.

Technology enters not as interruption, but as intensifier.

It is often spoken about as if it carries intention of its own. In practice, technology amplifies whatever logic already governs a system. Where extraction dominates, it accelerates extraction. Where fear shapes decisions, it spreads fear efficiently. Where ego seeks control, it scales control. Technology does not decide what is right. It repeats what is valued.

In small systems, coherence can be carried through personal relationship. Context is shared. Repair happens informally. As systems scale, this intimacy thins. Distance increases. Decisions are mediated. Technology steps in to compensate for speed, volume, and reach. At this point, technology ceases to be neutral. It becomes moral architecture—the structure through which values are enacted at scale.

Many people sense a quiet unease here. Not because technology is powerful, but because it often feels indifferent. Systems optimise without listening. Platforms reward attention without meaning. Algorithms shape behaviour without accountability. Speed overtakes reflection. This unease is not anti-technology. It is a recognition that intelligence without relationship becomes blind.

Soul is not lost because technology is cold.
It is lost when coherence is not encoded.

From an Altruian perspective, technology is an extension of human relationship—with time, attention, one another, and the future. Every design choice answers relational questions, whether or not they are named: Who is seen? Who decides? Who benefits? Who carries the cost? When these questions are ignored, harm scales invisibly. When they are held consciously, technology becomes a partner rather than a threat.

Scaling with soul therefore requires that technology serve continuity, not just growth. Continuity means relationships are not sacrificed for speed, learning is not erased by automation, nuance is not flattened by metrics, and people remain participants rather than data points. This does not reject automation. It insists that automation support human judgement rather than replace it.

Ethics in technology generally appear as defaults. What happens when someone makes a mistake? How easy is it to repair harm? What behaviour is subtly rewarded? What kind of attention is encouraged? What is made visible, and what disappears? These choices shape culture long before values are debated. Design, in this sense, becomes destiny.

Artificial intelligence intensifies this dynamic. AI does not generate values; it reflects patterns. It learns from what exists and extends it at scale. If trained on competition, it amplifies competition. If trained on bias, it reproduces bias. If trained on care, it can model care. *AI becomes dangerous not because it is intelligent, but because it is unconscious.* Without ethical orientation, it mirrors the worst of us with extraordinary efficiency. With ethical intelligence, it can help us see ourselves more clearly—and choose differently.

Technology aligned with Creative Altruism feels distinct. It supports cooperation without coercion. It increases transparency rather than control. It distributes value rather than concentrating it. People experience it as supportive rather than manipulative, enabling rather than extractive.

As tools grow more capable, a paradox emerges. The more we automate, the more valuable certain human capacities become. Listening. Discernment. Empathy. Ethical judgement. Creative synthesis. Relational intelligence. These are not inefficiencies to be optimised away. They are the very qualities that allow technology to be used wisely.

Leadership in technological environments therefore changes shape. It is less about mastering tools and more about holding coherence while tools accelerate everything else. Leaders are asked to remain accountable for outcomes even when decisions are mediated by code, to ask not only whether something works, but what it does to the field.

At a civilisational level, technology becomes a test. Not of capability, but of maturity. Humanity is learning whether it can build systems more powerful than itself without becoming less human. This is not a technical problem. It is a relational one.

The question is not whether technology will advance.
It will.

The question is whether our capacity for care, wisdom, and cooperation will advance alongside it. In many places, this movement has already begun—quietly, imperfectly, but recognisably. Platforms are being designed to reward contribution. Teams use tools to support transparency and shared learning. Communities experiment with technology that strengthens connection rather than replacing it.

Quiet Reprise
Technology amplifies intention.
Scale reveals values.
When intelligence is guided by care,
and speed is held by purpose,
the tools we build
do not strip us of our humanity—
they give it
room to endure.

CHAPTER 32

From Creative Altruism to Digital Creative Altruism

Creative Altruism does not change when it enters digital space. What changes is consequence. Under analogue conditions, intention often remained local. Care could be personal. Harm was limited by proximity. In digital conditions, scale alters everything. What was once a choice becomes a pattern. What was once an exception becomes a rule. What was once invisible becomes systemic.

Digital Creative Altruism names this shift.

It does not introduce a new philosophy. It describes Creative Altruism under conditions where creativity, cooperation, and value move through platforms, protocols, and systems that shape behaviour long before intention has time to act. Here, ethics cannot remain aspirational. They must become structural.

Digital systems do not host values.
They encode them.

Every platform carries assumptions about authorship, ownership, visibility, reward, and power. These assumptions are rarely announced, yet they shape outcomes relentlessly. What is rewarded repeats. What is ignored disappears. Under these conditions, goodwill alone is insufficient. Even sincere intentions are overridden when system logic accelerates faster than reflection.

Digital Creative Altruism begins from a simple recognition: when creativity moves through digital systems, altruism must move from attitude to architecture.

The question is no longer whether people mean well. It is whether systems make it easier to cooperate than to extract.

Attribution reveals this clearly. Digital creative work is rarely singular. Ideas emerge through influence, iteration, collaboration, and shared context. Yet attribution systems often collapse this richness into simplified narratives—a single author, a dominant brand, a powerful intermediary. At small scale, this feels unfair. At large scale, it becomes ethical harm.

Misattribution does more than deny credit. It severs relationship. It teaches participants that contribution leaks value rather than returning it. Over time, creativity contracts—not because people stop caring, but because care stops being viable.

Digital Creative Altruism treats attribution as ethics. To attribute well is not merely to name contributors, but to recognise participation as relational. When recognition flows proportionally, transparently, and reliably, creativity relaxes. People contribute more freely when they trust that their contribution will be seen.

Trust itself changes shape in digital environments. Familiarity can no longer carry it. Participants may never meet. Decisions may be mediated by code. Outcomes may unfold across time and geography. Trust therefore shifts from personality to visibility.

Transparency becomes infrastructure.

Not transparency as exposure or surveillance, but transparency as legibility—the ability to see how decisions are made, how value flows, how participation is recognised, and how imbalance is corrected. When systems are opaque, suspicion grows. When systems are legible, trust stabilises without effort.

Fairness, too, must evolve. In digital systems, fairness cannot depend solely on intention or discretion. It must become executable. When rules remain implicit, power concentrates. When justice relies on intervention, it arrives too late. Programmable fairness does not mean rigidity. It means embedding agreed principles into system behaviour so that fairness becomes default rather than exception.

Cooperation by design follows naturally from this shift. Most digital systems reward competition unintentionally. They privilege visibility over contribution, speed over care, scale over coherence. Even cooperative people begin to behave defensively—not because they lack goodwill, but because the environment trains them to do so.

Digital Creative Altruism asks a different design question: what would cooperation look like if the system itself favoured it?

When defaults are shaped so that sharing is easier than withholding, recognition easier than erasure, and participation more rewarding than extraction, altruism ceases to feel sacrificial. It becomes practical.

Every platform is a moral environment. Not because it declares values, but because it shapes behaviour. What it amplifies becomes culture. What it tolerates becomes normal. Ethics, here, is not ideology. It is consequence.

What emerges next is not only a different way of working together, but a different way of understanding value itself.

Quiet Reprise
Digital systems do not ask
what we believe.
They repeat
what we design.
When creativity moves at scale,
altruism must become structure—
or coherence dissolves.
Digital Creative Altruism
is not a future aspiration.
It is the minimum condition
for creativity
to remain human.

CHAPTER 33

Economies of Shared Purpose

Modern economies are extraordinarily efficient at producing goods, services, and growth. Yet they often struggle to produce meaning, cohesion, and long-term trust. As organisations scale, something subtle is frequently lost: a shared sense of purpose that binds effort to contribution, and contribution to the common good.

Creative Altruism does not reject economics. It reframes it.

At its heart lies a simple but transformative insight: when people cooperate in service of a shared purpose, value does not merely accumulate — it *compounds*. What emerges is not an alternative to economic activity, but a deeper logic beneath it: an economy shaped by shared purpose rather than narrow self-interest.

This chapter names a logic already at work, rather than proposing a new economic model.

SHARENOMICS: THE ECONOMICS OF SHARED PURPOSE AND SERVICE

Sharenomics describes the economies that arise when value is created, sustained, and shared through cooperation in service of a higher purpose. Rather than maximising extraction or short-term advantage, Sharenomics recognises that enduring value emerges from contribution, trust, and alignment.

In Sharenomics:

- Cooperation is not a concession, but a strategic advantage
- Service is not peripheral, but foundational
- Shared purpose becomes an organising force for economic activity

This is not an ideological proposal. It is an observation of how complex human systems behave when aligned around meaning. Where shared purpose is present, friction reduces. Where cooperation replaces zero-sum rivalry, resources are used more intelligently. Where contribution is recognised and fairly shared, commitment deepens.

Sharenomics does not deny individual initiative or reward. It reframes them within a wider ecology of value — one in which personal success and collective benefit are no longer in opposition.

COMPOUND POSITIVE IMPACT (CPI): HOW VALUE MULTIPLIES

The engine that powers Sharenomics is *Compound Positive Impact (CPI)*.

CPI describes the multiplier effect that occurs when purposeful service is undertaken cooperatively and guided by shared purpose. The initial act of service produces direct benefit — but it also triggers secondary and tertiary effects that amplify impact over time.

Participants experience:

- A sense of meaning, pride, and fulfilment
- Strengthened relationships and trust
- Reduced rivalry and softened prejudices
- A growing sense of belonging and shared identity

At the collective level, this leads to:

- Greater cohesion and resilience
- Enhanced creativity and collective intelligence
- Stronger reputational and relational capital
- Long-term economic and cultural value

These effects are not additive; they are *compounding*. Each cycle of cooperation strengthens the conditions for the next. Shared purpose reinforces trust. Trust enables deeper cooperation. Cooperation expands impact. Impact, in turn, renews purpose.

SHARING BY DESIGN

If Sharenomics is the economic context, and CPI the structural logic, then *Sharing by Design* is the principle that makes them durable.

Sharing by Design recognises that value distribution cannot be an afterthought. When sharing is left to goodwill alone, it remains fragile. When it is embedded into structures, processes, and agreements, it becomes resilient.

This does not imply equal outcomes, nor the absence of reward. It implies *fairness, transparency, and intentionality* in how value is recognised and circulated. When people trust that contribution will be acknowledged and shared appropriately, cooperation becomes sustainable rather than sacrificial.

Sharing by Design transforms generosity from a personal virtue into a collective capability.

JUSTSHARE: AN ILLUSTRATIVE EXPRESSION

Within this broader landscape, *JustShare* is one possible illustrative expression of Sharing by Design — a way of thinking about how contribution, value, and reward might be aligned more consciously.

JustShare is not presented here as a universal solution or prescribed system, but as an illustrative example of how the principles of Sharenomics and CPI may be applied in practice. It reflects an emerging recognition that fairness in value sharing is not merely ethical, but functional — essential to trust, motivation, and long-term cooperation.

Other expressions will emerge, shaped by context, culture, and technology. What matters is not the form, but the principle: value created together should be shared justly.

LOOKING AHEAD: THE EMERGENCE OF NEW INFRASTRUCTURES

As economies become more networked, creative, and interdependent, new forms of infrastructure will inevitably arise to support shared purpose and cooperative value creation. Some will be cultural, some organisational, some technological.

Creative Altruism does not seek to define these in advance. It establishes the *conditions* under which they can evolve wisely.

The future belongs not to systems that extract the most, but to those that enable contribution, recognise value fairly, and compound positive impact across human and economic domains. In this sense, service is no longer a moral accessory to business. It becomes a strategic and structural necessity.

An economy of shared purpose is not a distant ideal. It is already emerging — wherever people choose cooperation over rivalry, contribution over extraction, and shared benefit over narrow gain.

Quiet Reprise
When purpose is shared and service is cooperative, value multiplies.
When value is shared fairly, cooperation endures.
And when cooperation endures, economies begin to serve life — rather than the other way around.

CHAPTER 34

Economy as Ecology

When Value Learns to Circulate

When technology amplifies scale, it inevitably reshapes exchange. How time, energy, attention, creativity, and care move through systems determines not only economic outcomes, but social health. Economies are not abstract mechanisms. They are lived relationships—ways of deciding who contributes, who benefits, and what is valued.

To speak of economy is to speak of how life is supported, or strained.

Most people encounter the economy not through charts or policy, but through experience. Through the pressure of making ends meet. Through the satisfaction of meaningful work. Through the tension between effort and reward. Through the quiet, persistent question: *Is this fair?* Economic systems touch the nervous system. They shape whether people feel secure or anxious, valued or replaceable, capable of generosity or trapped in survival.

Traditional economic thinking has tended to treat systems as machines. Inputs go in. Outputs come out. Efficiency is maximised. Waste is externalised. But living systems do not behave like machines. They behave like organisms. They circulate energy. They regenerate resources. They require balance. When extraction exceeds renewal, collapse follows.

Seen this way, economies function more accurately as ecologies.

In extractive systems, value accumulates. It pools, concentrates, and hardens into power. In ecological systems, value circulates. It moves where it is needed. It returns to those who contribute. It regenerates capacity. Circulation is not charity. It is systemic health. Economies fail less from lack of value than from blocked flow.

This shift becomes visible first in how work is understood. Work ceases to be merely a means of survival and begins to be experienced as participation. People ask not only *What can I get?* but *How do I contribute— and how is that contribution recognised?* When recognition is reliable, effort relaxes. When dignity is preserved, motivation deepens. Work begins to feel like exchange with integrity.

Ownership also changes character. Ecological economies do not abolish ownership. They reframe it. Ownership becomes stewardship— the responsibility to care for what one holds and to allow its benefits to circulate. Wealth is not shamed, but it is no longer isolated from consequence. Assets are evaluated not only by what they produce, but by how they affect the wider system.

Trust emerges here as economic infrastructure. When trust is present, transaction costs drop. Cooperation accelerates. Innovation compounds. When trust erodes, systems compensate with surveillance, enforcement, and bureaucracy—each expensive, each draining. Trust cannot be commanded. It must be designed for through transparency, fair attribution, visible accountability, and reliable exchange.

Technology amplifies whichever economic logic it carries. When aligned with extraction, it accelerates inequality. When aligned with circulation, it enables fairness at scale. Digital systems now make it possible to track contribution, distribute value, and recognise participation with precision.

This does not guarantee justice, but it makes designed justice possible.

In ecological economies, the commons is central rather than peripheral. Shared resources—knowledge, culture, infrastructure, environment—are recognised as foundations of collective wellbeing. Caring for the commons is not altruism. It is foresight. When commons are protected, systems thrive. When they are depleted, everything suffers.

Economic life is also emotional life. Shame around money, fear of scarcity, guilt about success, anxiety about worth—these emotions are produced by systems that disconnect value from humanity. When economies are redesigned to honour contribution and circulation, emotional relationship to value begins to heal. Defensiveness softens. Generosity becomes possible. Creativity re-enters.

Over time, economic behaviour shapes culture. What is rewarded becomes normal. What circulates defines what matters. When economies reward care, creativity, and cooperation, these qualities extend beyond markets into education, governance, and daily life. Economy ceases to be a separate domain and becomes an expression of shared values.

The Altruian economy does not arrive as a model to impose. It emerges wherever exchange is designed with awareness, care, and intelligence. It appears in cooperatives and collectives, in transparent platforms, in fair attribution systems, in communities that share risk and reward. It is imperfect, adaptive, and alive.

Like all living systems, it grows through participation.

Quiet Reprise
An economy is a living story
about what we value
and how we care for one another.
When value is allowed to circulate,
when contribution is recognised,
and when trust is designed rather than assumed,
exchange becomes nourishment—
and prosperity begins to feel
like life
in motion.

CHAPTER 35

Ageing with Purpose

The Quiet Advantage of the Grey Foxes

We are living through a period of collective unease. Technologies accelerate faster than cultural understanding can keep pace. Professions once assumed stable are re-evaluated. Skills built patiently over decades are suddenly questioned. Attention turns toward speed, adaptability, and what can still compete under conditions of automation and scale.

Much of this conversation centres on youth.
It rarely pauses to consider something slower, quieter, and increasingly consequential.

Lived experience.

In an age shaped by artificial intelligence, the accumulated experience of older people—those we might affectionately call the *Grey Foxes*—is not becoming obsolete. It is becoming more difficult to replace.

Artificial intelligence can process information, recognise patterns, optimise systems, and generate outputs at scale. What it cannot do is live a life. It cannot carry the memory of failure and recovery across decades. It cannot sense how decisions echo through relationships over time. It cannot recognise when efficiency begins to erode dignity, or when speed quietly undermines trust. These forms of intelligence are learned only through consequence.

The value of the Grey Foxes lies not primarily in what they know, but in what they have become.

Through years of responsibility, compromise, care, misjudgement, repair, loss, reconciliation, and recalibration, many older people develop a deeply embodied literacy in human systems. This literacy is not theoretical. It appears as judgement without rigidity, timing without urgency, humour without dismissal, and restraint without withdrawal. It often goes unnamed, even by those who carry it.

In this sense, Creative Altruism matures naturally over a lifetime. What may begin earlier as instinct becomes, through experience, discernment—the capacity to read situations, sense consequence, and act with generosity and restraint at the same time. This capacity cannot be accelerated. It is learned by living.

One of the quiet misunderstandings of our time is the belief that wisdom is simply advanced knowledge. Wisdom, as it appears here, is relational. It is the ability to hold context, to sense what is not being said, to recognise when a system is technically successful but ethically hollow. It is the intelligence that notices when something *works* but does not *belong*.

As systems grow faster and more complex, this form of intelligence becomes more valuable, not less.

Many Grey Foxes develop *an intuitive sensitivity to group dynamics and collective atmosphere.* They sense when to step forward and when to step back, when to speak and when to hold silence, when leadership is required and when leadership must circulate. This sensitivity often expresses itself quietly, without claim or performance.

It is easy for such intelligence to be overlooked in cultures that reward visibility over depth. Yet it is precisely this capacity that stabilises systems under pressure.

Ageing with purpose is not about clinging to relevance.
It is about redistributing value.

Later life often brings a subtle shift in orientation. As the need to prove softens, concern for others deepens. As ambition loses urgency, contribution gains clarity. As identity becomes less performative, generosity becomes more natural. This shift is not universal, but it is common enough to be recognised across cultures and lives.

Many older people find themselves increasingly willing to share credit, mentor without expectation, support without visibility, and invest in futures they will not personally dominate. This is not withdrawal from life. It is a refinement of participation. What matters increasingly is whether one's presence strengthens the whole rather than advances the self.

In the context of Creative Altruism, this role is not peripheral.
It is foundational.

A society navigating artificial intelligence responsibly does not only need technical expertise. It needs elders who can hold context, model restraint, and protect dignity where speed would otherwise dominate. It needs people willing to say no—not from fear, but from discernment—to technologies, business models, and cultural patterns that are impressive yet misaligned with human flourishing.

Ageing with purpose also involves a different relationship with time. Cycles become visible. Patterns repeat. Urgency becomes negotiable. Not everything needs to be solved immediately. Not every opportunity should be taken. This temporal literacy brings steadiness into environments that might otherwise escalate toward unnecessary harm.

Learning when *not* to act becomes a form of service.

This restraint is not passivity. It is judgement refined by experience. It allows space for others to step forward. It protects processes from being rushed. It preserves dignity when pressure would erode it. In many contexts, simply being present—steady, attentive, unhurried—becomes a meaningful contribution.

As professional landscapes recalibrate, many traditional roles will disappear or transform. What intensifies instead is the need for interpretation, ethical framing, and stewardship. Grey Foxes are uniquely positioned to serve as mentors of context rather than technique, guardians of values within fast-moving systems, and intergenerational translators between speed and meaning.

Their task is not to outpace technology.
It is to out-human it.

This is where a quiet invitation appears.

To the Grey Foxes: the time does not ask you to withdraw, nor to compete on terms that no longer make sense. It asks something more precise. It asks you to step forward consciously as carriers of continuity—bringing discernment where there is excess, steadiness where there is volatility, and care where speed threatens coherence.

This stepping forward does not require a movement, a role, or a platform. It begins wherever you are—through mentoring, listening, holding space, questioning assumptions, protecting dignity, and modelling restraint without cynicism. The contribution is recognised not by title, but by effect.

Ageing with purpose is not about holding on.
It is about holding true.

When this role is allowed—personally and culturally—something stabilises. Wisdom re-enters decision-making. Care deepens without sentimentality. Short-term thinking is tempered. The future gains continuity with the past rather than severance from it.

Quiet Reprise
There comes a moment when speed no longer impresses
and certainty no longer convinces.
What remains is not urgency,
but orientation.
Ageing with purpose does not mean stepping aside.
It means stepping in—
with care refined by time,
judgement shaped by consequence,
and the quiet courage
to stand in complexity
without needing to dominate it.
Time does not only take.
It gives—
when what has been lived
is allowed to serve.

CHAPTER 36

Cool, Kind & Joyful

When What We Are Drawn To Begins to Change

Cultural change rarely begins with argument.
It begins with attraction.

Long before people agree on what is right, they sense what feels alive. Long before norms shift, desire shifts. Something that once carried glamour, status, or authority begins to feel strangely hollow, while something else—often quieter, less performative—begins to feel compelling.

Every age has its version of *cool*.

Cool is never trivial. It is a cultural signal. It shapes what people admire, imitate, and aspire toward. It teaches behaviour without instruction. It legitimises certain ways of being and quietly sidelines others. What is considered cool tells a generation what is safe to want.

In the late twentieth century, cool was often bound to power, detachment, and dominance. Wealth signalled success. Emotional distance suggested control. Competition was admired. The unencumbered individual became aspirational. This aesthetic did not arise by accident. It reflected a world organised around scarcity, rivalry, and the belief that hardness was required to survive.

That version of cool had consequences.

It normalised extraction.
It rewarded indifference.
It treated care as weakness and cooperation as naïveté.

And for a time, it worked—on its own terms.

But the conditions that produced it no longer hold.

In a deeply interconnected world, detachment is no longer strength. It becomes impractical. Distance slows understanding. Cynicism erodes trust. Power exercised without care destabilises systems rather than securing them. What once felt sharp now feels brittle. What once impressed now tires.

Something else is emerging in its place.

Cool begins to shift from distance to presence. From posturing to steadiness. From irony to sincerity. From dominance to grounded confidence. Increasingly, what draws people is not who wins hardest or speaks loudest, but who can listen without collapsing, act without performing, and remain human within pressure.

This shift is felt before it is explained.

Kindness, once treated as optional or sentimental, reveals itself as competence. In complex systems, kindness reduces friction. It keeps communication clean. It allows truth to be spoken without humiliation and disagreement without rupture. This is kindness with backbone— clear, bounded, and reliable.

Joy undergoes a similar transformation.

In extractive cultures, joy often appears as escape: a brief release before pressure resumes. But when cooperation is real—when effort aligns with meaning and care is embedded rather than displayed—joy takes on a different quality. It becomes quieter, steadier, and more durable.

This joy shows up as lightness in conversation, ease of collaboration, and shared humour that supports the work rather than interrupting it. People leave with energy rather than depletion. Time feels less pressured. Problems feel workable again. Joy, here, is not indulgence. It is coherence made emotional.

When cool, kind, and joyful begin to converge, cultural taste shifts.

Steadiness becomes attractive.
Sincerity gains credibility.
Care stops needing apology.

Play returns—not as distraction, but as social glue. Humour softens rigidity. Curiosity replaces defensiveness. Cooperation becomes something people want to participate in, not something they feel obliged to support.

This is how cultural movements actually form.

Not through persuasion.
Not through slogans.
But through preference.

For the Altruian Age to take root, Creative Altruism must not only be plausible or ethical. It must be habitable. It must feel good to be inside. It must show up naturally in language, creative work, education, enterprise, and everyday interaction.

This is not branding.
It is transmission.

Many people—especially younger generations—are already altruistically oriented. Empathy, fairness, and care come naturally. What is often missing is permission: permission to be openly kind without irony, to care without embarrassment, to cooperate without appearing naïve.

The role of Altruians is not to convince.
It is to embody.

To make creative altruism visible, enjoyable, and culturally legible. To create environments where people feel proud of their care rather than guarded about it. Where seriousness and lightness coexist. Where people belong without performance.

Creative Altruism does not spread by argument.
It spreads by atmosphere.

When people experience spaces that are calm without being passive, joyful without being frivolous, and kind without being weak, something in them recognises the difference. They want to stay. They want to return. They want to build from there.

This is how the new cool takes shape—quietly, relationally, and without announcement.

Not as a trend.
Not as a pose.
But as a way of being that feels more workable, more humane, and fully alive.

Quiet Reprise
What we are drawn to
reveals what we are becoming.
As cooperation settles into the ordinary,
cool warms,
kindness steadies,
and joy returns—
not as performance,
but as presence.
Not as escape,
but as shared aliveness.
Creative Altruism does not ask to be admired.
It invites us to enjoy
working well together—
and to discover
that this, too,
is a form of intelligence.

CHAPTER 37

Culture and the Art of Harmony

When Difference Learns How to Belong

Culture is rarely announced. It is felt.

What people are drawn to—what feels welcoming, workable, or quietly right—begins shaping culture long before it is named or understood.

You sense it the moment you enter a space—in the ease or tension of conversation, in how people greet one another without thinking about it. Long before words explain what is acceptable, culture teaches how to behave.

Most people recognise immediately when a place feels right. The body relaxes. Attention widens. Speech becomes less guarded. Nothing explicit signals safety, yet something responds. This response is embodied rather than intellectual. The nervous system registers coherence before the mind names it. Culture works at this level. It is shaped less by declarations than by repeated moments—how tension is met, how power is exercised, how mistakes are handled.

Culture is not something to be engineered. It is an atmosphere that forms through relationship, and harmony is the intelligence that allows difference to remain connected.

Harmony is often misunderstood as smoothness or sameness. As politeness, or the absence of disagreement. Lived harmony feels different. It has texture. It holds contrast. It allows disagreement without rupture. Harmony appears when difference is not eliminated, but related—when opposing perspectives can remain in conversation without collapsing into uniformity or fracture.

In this sense, harmony is dynamic. It listens, adjusts, and moves. It is not the absence of tension, but the capacity to work with it.

Where harmony is alive, difference feels safe. People do not rush to defend their position or dominate conversation in order to remain visible. They trust that their perspective can be expressed without penalty, even if it does not prevail. This trust does not emerge magically. It grows from experience—moments when dissent was met with curiosity rather than punishment, when disagreement did not cost belonging.

Every culture has a sound. Some feel loud even when quiet, charged with unspoken tension. Others feel muted, as if voices have learned to stay small. Some feel sharp, others diffuse. And some feel balanced. In balanced cultures, conversation breathes. Laughter appears naturally. Silence carries meaning rather than discomfort. Energy circulates instead of pooling in corners.

The true test of harmony appears under pressure. When time is short, stakes are high, or mistakes are costly, culture reveals what it actually is. Can people slow down enough to listen? Can truth be spoken without blame? Can authority be exercised without humiliation? Can care remain present without sacrificing clarity?

Cultures that hold harmony here earn trust. Those that cannot eventually fracture, even if they appear functional on the surface.

Pressure does not create culture. It exposes it.

Care is central to this capacity. Care is not softness. In harmonious cultures, care is precise. It shows up as attention to timing, tone, and impact. It shapes how boundaries are set and how responsibility is held. Care allows honesty to land. It makes repair possible. Without care, harmony becomes brittle. With it, even sharp differences can remain connected.

Harmony is not permanent. It requires tending. People misstep. Intentions are misunderstood. What matters is not avoidance, but response. In cultures where harmony is alive, repair is normal. Apologies are not humiliating. Clarification is welcomed. Returning to relationship is valued more than being right. Over time, this becomes a shared skill.

When cultural coherence stabilises, it becomes visible. People bring more of themselves. They take creative risks. They protect the space together. Outsiders feel it immediately, even if they cannot explain why. This beauty is not aesthetic alone. It is ethical. It is the visible expression of dignity held in relationship.

Culture teaches without instruction. It shapes character more powerfully than rules ever could. People become different simply by participating. This is why the art of harmony matters. It shapes not only outcomes, but who people become together.

Those who live inside a harmonious culture often forget how unusual it is. Only when they leave do they notice the contrast—the sharpness elsewhere, the constant negotiation of safety, the exhaustion of guarding.

Harmony, once experienced, becomes recognisable. People begin seeking it—not as perfection, but as coherence.

Quiet Reprise
Culture speaks
before words arrive.
When difference is met with care,
and tension is held without fear,
harmony does not need to be named—
it is felt,
and it teaches us
how to belong
without becoming the same.

CHAPTER 38

The Spiritual Present

When Inner Coherence Becomes Ordinary

Something quietly subtle is taking place—not in temples or movements, not through declarations or doctrines, but in the texture of everyday life. People are relating to the inner dimension differently. Less as belief to be asserted, less as identity to perform, and less as something to be explained or displayed. More as a quality of presence that quietly shapes how they live, decide, and relate.

For many, spirituality no longer arrives through language. It shows up in simpler, more grounded ways: the ability to pause before reacting, the choice to act with integrity when no one is watching. It appears in how people hold complexity, how they remain human under pressure, how they return to what matters after being pulled off course. It is coherence lived from the inside.

Belief once organised spiritual life. It offered certainty, structure, and belonging. For a long time, this served. But belief alone no longer holds what many are encountering. The world has become too interconnected, too visibly shaped by consequence. Certainty collapses under lived contradiction. Doctrine thins when experience grows nuanced.

People are learning to trust experience over explanation, presence over position. Spirituality shifts from what one holds to how one holds.

Inner coherence sits at the centre of this shift. It is not mystical. It is the felt alignment between thought, feeling, intention, and action. When these dimensions remain in conversation rather than conflict, life simplifies, and people stop arguing internally and begin acting without splitting themselves.

This coherence is lived before it is named.

What changes most is where spirituality lives. Not apart from life, but inside it. In conversations, in work, in listening, and in silence that carries meaning rather than discomfort. Presence is recognised not as a special state, but as the baseline that makes everything else workable. It is not passive. It is active attentiveness.

As spirituality becomes lived, ethics deepen—not as rules to follow, but as sensitivity to impact. People notice more quickly when their actions fragment trust, and they adjust, not out of guilt, but out of alignment. Ethical maturity appears quietly: choosing repair over defence, responsibility over blame, restraint over excess, honesty over performance. These choices are rarely dramatic. They are made in small moments where character reveals itself.

One of the clearest signs of this shift is what is falling away. The spiritual persona. The need to appear evolved. The subtle superiority disguised as insight. People are less drawn to those who speak about consciousness and more to those who embody steadiness, humility, and care. Depth becomes recognisable through behaviour. Spirituality, stripped of display, becomes trustworthy again.

Stillness returns in a new form—not as withdrawal, but as orientation. People touch stillness briefly and often rather than chasing peak experience. A breath. A pause. A moment of attention. Stillness becomes calibration, allowing emotion to settle and intention to clarify. From stillness, action becomes cleaner.

This inner shift does not remain private. A person who is internally coherent changes the field around them. They regulate tension. They listen without fear. As more people live this way, environments soften. Conflicts resolve sooner. Inner coherence becomes a collective resource.

Perhaps most importantly, this spirituality does not seek escape. There is less interest in leaving the world behind and more commitment to inhabiting it fully. Less longing for transcendence, more willingness to stand within complexity without collapsing. This is not renunciation. It is maturity.

Those living inside this shift often struggle to name it. They simply notice that life feels less performative, values feel lived rather than stated, care feels structural rather than sentimental, and meaning feels close at hand. The inner life no longer needs to be separate from the outer one.

Nothing here rejects what came before. What endures in earlier spiritual traditions—attention, humility, service, presence—remains vital. What falls away are forms that no longer support lived coherence. Spiritual life continues not by repeating structures, but by carrying essence forward.

This movement is incomplete, uneven, and quiet. It does not announce itself or seek followers. It simply lives—in how people pause, choose, and return to what matters without needing to name it.

Quiet Reprise
Spiritual life no longer asks
to be believed.
It asks to be lived—
in how we pause,
in how we choose,
in how we return
to what matters
without needing
to say its name.

CHAPTER 39

The Quiet Continuation

Where the Work No Longer Needs a Name

There is a moment, often unnoticed, when a way of thinking completes its task. Not because it has been exhausted, but because it has been absorbed. The language loosens. The concepts relax their grip. What remains is not conclusion, but continuity—the sense that life knows how to carry forward what has been recognised.

Creative Altruism was never meant to become a doctrine, a system to be defended, or an identity to inhabit. It names an orientation already underway: the gradual rebalancing of human intelligence toward cooperation, care, and coherence in conditions where force no longer works. Once this orientation is felt, it no longer needs reinforcement. It becomes a reference point—quiet, available, and sufficient.

What continues is not an idea, but a way of standing. It is a way of standing that listens more than it asserts, and keeps space for what has not yet found language.

At a certain point, the work stops feeling novel. The language becomes familiar. The practices feel ordinary. Inner and outer life no longer need constant negotiation. People notice that they are no longer arguing themselves into coherence. They are living it—imperfectly, attentively, and with increasing ease.

This is not idealism.
It is practicality refined.

A new way of being does not arrive through instruction. It appears when effort softens and alignment remains. People act with awareness of consequence, not because they are trying to be ethical, but because coherence feels better than fragmentation.

Belonging shifts meaning here.
It no longer depends on similarity or agreement.
It arises through participation.

People belong because they show up with care, listen without fear, and remain present when things are uncomfortable. Difference remains. So does dignity. What changes is the field in which difference is held.

The distinction between inner work and outer action begins to dissolve. Reflection informs behaviour. Behaviour informs understanding. Presence stabilises both.

Purpose becomes less something one pursues and more something one recognises in how one participates.

This way of being carries a distinct rhythm. Nothing is rushed. Nothing is withheld. Over time, this rhythm protects against burnout and brittleness. Effort becomes sustainable because it is not driven by fear or performance.

Joy appears naturally here—not as reward, but as by-product. The joy of work that matters. Of relationships that can hold truth. This joy is quieter than excitement, but more reliable. It does not depend on outcome. It accompanies coherence.

The world does not need more answers.

It needs more people who can remain present inside uncertainty.

This presence has consequences. It changes how conflict unfolds, how systems are designed, how power is exercised, how technology is shaped, how value circulates. None of this requires agreement on belief or allegiance to a movement. It requires only enough people choosing coherence often enough that it becomes normal.

Creative Altruism, in this sense, does not promise resolution. It offers relationship. It does not offer certainty. It offers coherence.

When care, creativity, and cooperation remain in relationship, the work continues without needing a name.

The future shaped by this orientation will not look uniform. It will express itself differently across cultures, communities, and lives. What remains consistent is quality: care that does not collapse into sentiment, creativity that does not detach from consequence, cooperation that does not erase difference, and purpose that does not harden into ideology.

These qualities endure because they adapt.

The work ahead does not require agreement or allegiance. It asks only for attention — renewed as needed — to what strengthens coherence and what diminishes it. Civilisations do not turn through grand gestures or decisive moments. They turn through accumulated choices that feel ordinary while they are being made: how people listen, how they decide, how they respond when pressure rises. When coherence becomes familiar in these small ways, the work no longer needs direction or defence. It continues quietly, wherever it is allowed to live.

Quiet Reprise
Nothing needs to be carried forward
except attention.
When coherence becomes ordinary,
the world does not change all at once—
but it begins, quietly,
to recognise itself
in how we live.

CHAPTER 40

The Book, the Ecosystem, and the Invitation

This book is not a destination.
It is a point of orientation.

What has been explored here does not ask to be adopted, defended, or carried forward intact. It offers language for recognising patterns that many people already encounter in their lives and work — moments when creativity, care, and cooperation remain in relationship long enough to matter.

The intention of *The Art of Creative Altruism* has been to clarify perception rather than prescribe action. To name what becomes visible when force recedes and attention returns. To offer a shared vocabulary for coherence without turning that vocabulary into a system or an identity.

What has been named here — integration, shared belief, field awareness, the individual, team, and community paths, and the implications for technology and economy — does not resolve itself through agreement or understanding alone. These ideas come alive only when tested in real contexts, with real people, under real conditions.

This is where application begins — not as implementation, but as encounter.

Alongside the book, an ecosystem of practice is gradually taking shape. Not as a finished organisation or a defined institution, but as an evolving field of exploration. A place where the questions raised here can be tested, adapted, and sometimes set aside in response to lived reality.

Where the book offers orientation, the ecosystem explores application. Where the book names principles, the ecosystem encounters consequence. Where the book holds ethical direction, the ecosystem remains accountable to what actually works.

The ecosystem exists not to extend the book, but to continue the inquiry it opens.

Some readers will carry these ideas quietly into their own lives and work, changing nothing outwardly while something essential reorganises inwardly. Others will recognise a desire to explore more actively — through collaboration, experimentation, or shared learning. Neither response is privileged.

There is no requirement to participate.
No need to agree.
No obligation to carry the language forward.

What matters is how each person stands inside the situations they already inhabit.

If Creative Altruism continues, it will not do so because of this book, or because of any ecosystem that gathers around it. It will continue wherever people choose — again and again — to meet complexity with care, to design for cooperation rather than extraction, and to act with integrity even when outcomes are uncertain.

This book has offered ground.
The ecosystem offers places where that ground can be met.

What follows belongs neither to the text nor to its author. It unfolds through attention, relationship, and the quiet courage to participate in what is already becoming.

What Continues

When a book ends, something often resolves. An argument closes. A position is secured. A set of ideas is brought to rest.

This book does not ask for that kind of ending.

What continues here is not a conclusion, but an orientation — a way of noticing what strengthens coherence and what erodes it, across situations that rarely announce themselves as significant at the time. Often, this noticing takes the form of listening rather than speaking, and of allowing meaning to arrive rather than insisting it be resolved.

If *The Art of Creative Altruism* has served its purpose, it has not done so by persuading or instructing. It has offered language for experiences many people already recognise: moments when cooperation feels more intelligent than force, when care stabilises rather than weakens, and when creativity emerges not from pressure, but from relationship.

You will not encounter Creative Altruism as a doctrine or a movement. You will encounter it in ordinary situations — in a conversation that shifts because someone listens fully, in a decision that feels cleaner because impact is considered, in a system that begins to work more humanely because contribution is recognised and allowed to circulate.

Such moments do not announce themselves as altruistic.
They simply feel workable.

The conditions that shape contemporary life — complexity, speed, interdependence — are unlikely to recede. What changes is how they are met. The question is no longer how to avoid these conditions, but how to remain coherent within them without losing dignity, relationship, or meaning.

What carries forward is not language or framework, but practice: the quiet ways people choose tone, timing, and attention; the moments when restraint proves more effective than escalation; the decisions to cooperate where extraction once seemed easier. No system is neutral. What is practised repeatedly becomes structure. What is embodied becomes transmissible.

This is how the work continues — not through allegiance or advocacy, but through participation.

There is no call to action here, and no requirement to remember what has been written. What matters is what remains available when you find yourself at a threshold: the capacity to pause, to notice, and to choose what strengthens coherence rather than fragments it.

If something in these pages has felt familiar rather than convincing, if it has named what you have already sensed but not yet articulated, then the work is already underway — quietly, imperfectly, and without ownership.

And that is enough to keep the field open.

Defining Creative Altruism

Creative Altruism refers to an orientation in which creativity, care, and cooperation operate together in service of the greater good.

Rather than treating creativity as individual talent or altruism as moral self-sacrifice, Creative Altruism understands both as relational capacities embedded within human systems. It describes a way of engaging the world in which ingenuity is guided by ethical awareness, and cooperation becomes a practical intelligence rather than a concession.

This definition is descriptive rather than prescriptive. It offers language for recognising patterns of coherence already observable in cultural, organisational, technological, and social domains.

BEHAVIOURAL FRAMING

In some contexts, Creative Altruism is defined primarily as the intentional use of creativity and compassion in service to others. This framing emphasises observable action: creative problem-solving directed toward reducing harm, strengthening communities, or improving collective wellbeing.

This behavioural interpretation is clear and accessible. It highlights service, innovation, and compassionate contribution as visible expressions of Creative Altruism.

Its strength lies in describing what Creative Altruism looks like in action.

ORIENTATIONAL FRAMING

In this book, Creative Altruism is approached not only as behaviour, but as orientation.

Here it is treated as a cultivated literacy: the capacity to perceive, navigate, and design relational systems so that creativity, care, and cooperation remain aligned under conditions of complexity.

A literacy is not a personality trait. It is a learnable capacity. Just as textual literacy enables participation in written culture, Creative Altruism enables participation in complex human systems without fragmentation.

In this framing, action arises from orientation. Behaviour becomes the expression of inner and systemic coherence.

INTEGRATION OF BOTH PERSPECTIVES

The behavioural and orientational interpretations are not opposed.

The behavioural framing clarifies what Creative Altruism does.
The orientational framing clarifies what makes it sustainable.

Service without coherence risks performance.
Coherence without service risks abstraction.

When orientation and action remain in relationship, Creative Altruism becomes durable.

It is, at once, a way of being and a way of acting.

Creative Altruism is not owned. It is stewarded. Its articulation will continue to evolve across cultures and contexts. What remains constant is relational quality: creativity guided by care, cooperation embedded in structure, and contribution aligned with continuity.

When these remain in conversation, the term fulfils its function.

When they do not, it becomes unnecessary.

ABOUT THE AUTHOR

Reza Riezouw's professional life has spanned art and culture, media and entertainment, travel and maritime operations, estate and asset management, family office advisory, high technology leadership, and strategic brand development. Over several decades, he has worked across entrepreneurial ventures, governance roles, and creative industries, navigating the intersection of economic systems, cultural expression, and leadership responsibility.

Alongside his professional path, Reza has maintained a lifelong contemplative practice and sustained engagement with philosophical, metaphysical, and spiritual traditions across cultures. His inquiry has consistently centred on questions of meaning, cooperation, and the relationship between inner development and outer structures.

Creative Altruism emerged from the convergence of these lived experiences and reflections. His work brings together cross-cultural experience and philosophical inquiry into a coherent framework exploring creativity, care, and cooperation as foundational principles for meaningful work and cultural evolution — articulated as an applied contemporary philosophy for a shifting world.

He does not present himself as the originator of a doctrine, but as an articulator and steward of ideas whose relevance he believes is becoming increasingly evident in a world seeking more humane and cooperative forms of organisation. This book reflects lived engagement rather than biographical assertion, and is offered in service of a shared human inquiry.

Reza Riezouw was born in Iran to a Persian mother and Dutch father, and educated in Europe. He lives in Porto with his wife, who has been an active partner in every dimension of the life, work, and study that has shaped this book. Their three grown children are active in the creative industries and continue to provide the inspiration, challenge, and insight that keep his work grounded and responsive.

ACKNOWLEDGEMENTS

This work has been shaped by many influences — personal, intellectual, and cultural — and by conversations that extend far beyond the author. It draws upon traditions of thought, lived experience, and shared inquiry that cannot be traced to any single source or individual.

Gratitude is due to those whose ideas, actions, and examples — whether encountered directly or indirectly — have contributed to the questions explored in these pages. Particular thanks are offered to family, friends, collaborators, and fellow practitioners who have supported the work through dialogue, encouragement, and challenge.

I am also deeply grateful to the city of Porto, and to the quiet generosity, humour, and soulful steadiness of its people, whose presence has shaped the conditions in which this work could take form.

Above all, this book acknowledges the wider human effort to understand how creativity, care, and cooperation might be more consciously woven into our lives and institutions. If it succeeds in any measure, it does so as part of that collective endeavour.

GLOSSARY OF KEY TERMS

AGE OF AQUARIUS

A symbolic cultural lens associated with participation, decentralisation, shared intelligence, and relational awareness. Used descriptively in this book to name shifts in collective orientation under conditions of complexity and interdependence.

AGE OF PISCES

A symbolic cultural lens associated with faith, hierarchy, sacrifice, and externally mediated meaning. Referenced descriptively rather than literally.

ALTRUIA

The conceptual and relational field within which Creative Altruism is explored and lived. Altruia refers primarily to an orientation or state of participation — an atmosphere shaped by creativity, care, and cooperation — rather than to a fixed institution or program.

ALTRUIA ORGANISATION

A proposed future structural expression distinct from Altruia as orientation. It refers to a potential institutional framework through which the principles of Creative Altruism may be translated into programs, structures, and collaborative initiatives. Its development remains open and evolutionary rather than predetermined.

ALTRUIAN

A person, organisation, or system operating in alignment with contribution, cooperation, and coherence. The term denotes orientation rather than identity.

ALTRUIAN AGE

A descriptive term for an emerging civilisational orientation in which altruism becomes structural rather than exceptional, and cooperation becomes a core competence under conditions of complexity.

ALTRUIAN ETHIC

A lived atmosphere of coherence arising when commitments and agreements are practised reliably. Not a moral code, but an embodied pattern of clarity, listening, fairness, and service.

ALTRUIAN FIELD

A coherent relational atmosphere generated when purpose, care, and intelligence remain in alignment across individuals and systems, enabling collective intelligence and trust.

ALTRUISTIC ARTIFICIAL INTELLIGENCE (AAI)

Artificial intelligence shaped by principles of cooperation, care, and shared benefit. Emphasises ethical consequence and relational intelligence rather than optimisation for extraction or dominance.

ATTRIBUTION

The ethical recognition of contribution as relational and layered rather than singular. Designed attribution supports trust and sustainable creativity.

CARE

Relational intelligence that stabilises systems, preserves dignity, and allows complexity to remain workable. Structural care becomes competence.

COHERENCE

The felt integrity that arises when elements fit together in alignment. Recognised experientially as clarity, ease, and reduced friction.

COLLECTIVE INTELLIGENCE

Intelligence that emerges between people when presence, trust, and shared purpose allow ideas to build rather than compete.

COMMITMENT

An inner decision to return repeatedly to a chosen quality of presence or behaviour, especially under pressure. The foundation of culture.

CREATIVE ALTRUISM

Creativity, care, and cooperation working together for the greater good. Not a virtue or ideology, but a cultivated literacy enabling coherent participation in complex human systems.

CREATIVE COOPERATION

Cooperation that preserves difference while arranging it intelligently. Not consensus, but orchestration.

DIGITAL CREATIVE ALTRUISM

Creative Altruism under digital conditions, where ethics must move from intention to architecture because systems encode values at scale.

EMPATHY

An innate human capacity that, in Creative Altruism, extends beyond recognising pain to sensing orientation—what is needed, emerging, or possible—while preserving dignity and agency.

FIELD

The relational atmosphere that forms wherever people interact. Shaped by tone, trust, clarity, and presence. Includes the practices of field listening and field stewardship.

INTEGRATION

The quiet intelligence by which diverse elements move as one without losing uniqueness. The keystone of sustainable cooperation.

JUSTSHARE

A principle of designing systems so that value created together returns fairly and transparently to contributors. An illustrative expression of sharing by design.

KIND HONESTY

Truth spoken without weaponisation and care expressed without avoidance. Maintains clarity without humiliation.

LEADERSHIP (ALTRUIAN)

The capacity to hold coherence rather than control outcomes. Field-sensitive, responsive, and oriented toward service and renewal.

MARGINALIA

Fragments or partial expressions that invite participation rather than closure. In Creative Altruism, unfinished thought is treated as contribution.

MATURE CONSCIOUSNESS

An integrated developmental state in which cognitive clarity, emotional steadiness, ethical orientation, and relational awareness function coherently. Creativity and responsibility arise beyond self-protection.

PRECESSION OF THE EQUINOXES

A slow astronomical phenomenon used symbolically in cultural discourse to name long-term shifts in collective orientation.

PRESENCE

The ability to remain here—internally and relationally—without fragmentation. Allows response rather than reaction.

PURPOSE

Alignment rather than ambition. The organising gravity that reduces friction and directs attention toward contribution.

RAY STRUCTURE

The composite pattern through which different human qualities (the Seven Rays) express across individuals and systems.

SEVEN RAYS

A symbolic grammar describing seven recurring qualities of human and systemic expression. Used as a pattern language rather than an identity system.

SHARED BELIEF

A lived atmosphere of meaning carried in behaviour rather than doctrine. Stabilises cooperation under uncertainty.

SILENCE KEEPING

The ethical practice of restraint in communication—protecting space for listening, emergence, and coherence.

SPIRITUALITY (ALTRUIAN)

Inner coherence between thought, feeling, intention, and action. Lived alignment rather than belief or display.

THRESHOLD

A moment where attention shifts and choice becomes possible again. Regulates rhythm without stopping movement.

TRANSPARENCY

Legibility of decision-making, participation, and value flows. A structural foundation of trust.

TRUTH

Shared respect for reality rather than certainty or ideology. A precondition for trust and cooperation.

WAYFINDING

Navigation through uncertainty guided by coherence rather than fixed maps. Relies on orientation, rhythm, and learning.

PUBLISHER'S NOTE

The Art of Creative Altruism is intended as a foundation.

It offers language, orientation, and a shared ethical ground for a way of working, creating, and cooperating that is still emerging. No single volume can fully explore the many dimensions of this field.

In time, Altruia may publish further works that explore specific aspects of Creative Altruism more deeply—such as cooperation, ageing with purpose, storytelling, technology, and other domains where creativity, care, and cooperation intersect. These publications are not sequels, but companion explorations—each standing on its own while contributing to a shared field of practice.

altruiapress.com